East of Eden: New Romanian Plays

East of Eden: New Romanian Plays

Edited by Andrei Marinescu

Carysfort Press, Dublin

A Carysfort Press Book in association with Peter Lang

East of Eden: New Romanian Plays

Edited by Andrei Marinescu
First published in Ireland in 2005 as a paperback original by Carysfort Press, 58 Woodfield, Scholarstown Road, Dublin 16, Ireland

Typeset by Carysfort Press
Cover design by Alan Bennis

ISBN 978-1-78874-970-1

This publication has been supported by a Title by Title grant from the Arts Council and by a grant from the Ireland Literature Exchange. The translation project was supported by the Stewart Parker Trust and the Ireland Romania Cultural Foundation.

for John Fairleigh

Contents

Acknowledgements
Writers
Foreword
Editor's Preface

East of Eden: New Romanian Plays

Bones for Otto
By Lia Bugnar
Translated by Andrei Marinescu
Adapted by Michael Collins 1

Insomniacs: The Far Side of the Accordion
By Mimi Branescu
Translated by Andrei Marinescu
Adapted by Christian O'Reilly 24

Our Father Who Art in the Supermarket
By Petre Barbu
Translated by Andrei Marinescu
Adapted by Paul Meade 88

Stop the Tempo!
By Gianina Cărbunariu
Translated by Andrei Marinescu
Adapted by Paul Meade 150

Acknowledgements

The editor and colleagues would like to express their gratitude to the following:

Ovidiu Barbulescu, Catherine Boothman, Roxana Crisan, Alexandru Dabija,Vallejo Gantner, Marcel Iures, Siobhan O'Beirne, Emer O'Kelly, Sheila Pratschke, Stefan Tiron, Willie White, and Enid Reid Whyte.

Thanks are due to Uniter, the Romanian theatre union.

Writers

Petre Barbu: Born in Galati in 1962. He graduated from Mechanical Engineering Faculty in Galati. Senior Editor of *Capital* magazine. He made his literary debut in 1993, with a volume of short stories *The Orange Shirt* (Cartea Romaneasca Publishing House). He also published two novels, *God Bless America* and *The Last Outbreak of the Legionary Submarine* (both for Nemira Publishing House, 1995 and 1998). For his first play, *God Bless America*, he received the Camil Petrescu Award in 1997. Two other plays, *Left of the Father* and *The Duellist*, were nominated for Best New Play at the Uniter Gala, in 1998 and 2000. He finally received the prize in 2002 for *Our Father Who Art in the Supermarket.*

Mimi Branescu: Born in 1974 in Lehliu, in the Calarasi region of Romania. He studied acting at the Bucharest Theatre and Film Academy. As an actor, his most important creations include Lucentio in *Taming of the Shrew* by William Shakespeare (Bulandra Theatre); Bottom in *Midsummer Night's Dream* by William Shakespeare (Resita Theatre); Jerry in *Zoo Story* by Edward Albee (Targoviste Theatre); Valerio in *Leonce and Lena* by Georg Büchner (Targoviste Theatre). His first play, *The*

Garbage Man, was produced in 2003 by the Act Theatre in Bucharest and by the Fanny Tardini Theatre in Galati. Other plays he has written include *Hair Curlers* (produced by the Nottara Theatre in Bucharest), *The Dragons* and *The Panel at the End of the Bed* (produced by the Maria Filotti Theatre in Braila). He also worked as a film actor in *A Pack of Kent and a Pack of Coffee*, directed by Cristi Puiu (Golden Bear in Berlin, 2004), and in *Filantropica*, directed by Nae Caranfil.

Lia Bugnar: Born in 1969. She studied acting at the Bucharest Theatre and Film Academy. She has played numerous characters in theatre and cinema. Her most successful plays include *You Can't Feel It Here* and *Bones for Otto*, both of them produced by Green Hours Theatre in Bucharest. The two productions were invited to be performed at the Dublin Fringe Festival in 2004, where the company received the Project-Fringe Award.

Gianina Cărbunariu: Graduated in directing from the Bucharest Theatre and Film Academy in 2004. One of the initiators of DramAcum project for the support of Romanian playwriting. As a director, she is best known for *Stop the Tempo!* (also written by her) at the Green Hours Theatre in Bucharest and *Luck Helps Those Who Dare* by Xavier Kroetz, at the Act Theatre in Bucharest. She made her debut as a playwright with *Adventures from the Wild East.* Her most recent play, *mady-baby.edu*, was premiered early in 2005 at the Little Theatre in Bucharest, under her direction. The play was created during a residency at the Royal Court Theatre in London in the summer of 2004

Michael Collins: Before turning his hand to playwriting Michael Collins studied Engineering at Dublin City University. His plays include *The Hackney Office* (Druid Theatre Company, 2001) and *Tadhg Stray Wandered In* (Fishamble Theatre

Company, 2004). He is currently working on a new play for Rough Magic Theatre Company.

Paul Meade: Writer, director, and actor and joint Artistic Director of Guna Nua Theatre Company. Previous work includes the plays, *Skin Deep* (winner Stewart Parker Award 2004) and *Scenes From a Water Cooler* (with David Parnell, winner Best Production Dublin Fringe 2001) and the translation of *All These Guys* by Gianina Cărbinariu. Paul is from Limerick and studied acting at Trinity College and holds a M.A. in Modern Drama from U.C.D.

Christian O'Reilly: A Listowel writer who writes for theatre, television, film and radio. Druid have produced two of his plays: *It Just Came Out* and *The Good Father*, directed by Garry Hynes and joint winner of the 2002 Stewart Parker Award. Screenwriting credits include the award winning film *Inside I'm Dancing*, which is based on his original story.

Foreword

By Fiach MacConghail
Artistic Director of the Abbey, the National Theatre of Ireland

Since it was founded in 1904 by the writers W.B. Yeats and Augusta Gregory the Abbey Theatre has defined itself by the new work it has presented. And it is not too fanciful to suggest that a history of this Abbey repertoire is a fair reflection of Ireland's journey through the twentieth century. The early productions of plays by Yeats and Gregory and the writers they gathered around them helped to build a confident and separate cultural identity as the country moved towards independence; but as Ireland settled into a conservative alliance between the new state and the church, it was on the Abbey stage that this emerging constraint on individual expression was challenged. Facing official condemnation and even riots in the theatre, the Abbey encouraged writers such as Sean O'Casey and John Millington Synge to openly examine the mythologies of Irish society ancient and modern.

Into its second hundred years, the Abbey will support and provide a creative context for all theatre artists. However, it still sees itself as a literary theatre, with its playwrights a voice expressing and questioning modern Irish identity; names like Brian Friel, Tom Murphy, Marina Carr and Sebastian Barry must be the cornerstone of any programming, but the theatre needs also to be fed through the root by the imagination and unorthodoxy of each new and emerging generation.

The Abbey, like any National Theatre, wants to draw these young writers around and to support them towards productions on home ground. But it wants also to nourish itself, no less than its writers, from the energies and innovations of other theatre traditions. We draw much of our reputation from the great texts we have contributed to the international repertoire, while Romania is respected worldwide for a distinctively visual style of presentation and direction. It seems like an attractive and symbiotic relationship to be developed.

Younger Irish writers such as Malachy McKenna, Conor McPherson, Eugene O'Brien and Gerard Stembridge have been introduced to Romanian readers and audiences through the first anthology edited by critic and translator Andrei Marinescu. Now we have this companion volume of four new Romanian plays in English versions, and the exchange of texts and creative talent grows apace. Keep it all going!

Foreword

Ion Caramitru
General Director of the National Theatre, Bucharest

Young playwrights must try to demolish the pre-established theatre system, to be shocking and to fight in order to impose themselves – without this principle theatre cannot evolve. And this is why we must not spare any effort in helping talented new writers such as the ones included in the present anthology, some of them taking the first steps in a career that requires many sacrifices and frustrations.

The National Theatre in Bucharest is planning to focus its repertoire not only on re-discovering and bringing to life old Romanian theatre plays of indisputable value, but also on developing this young dramaturgical wave which we need to refresh the Romanian theatre space.

We must never forget that one of the basic duties of theatre is to sustain a permanent opposition to the conformist tendency of society. Before the fall of the communist regime in 1989, the theatre was not able to tell the truth to the people in a direct way; the audiences were filling the theatres to inhale a hidden message, based mostly on the power of allusion. But today we must regain the desire and the ability to express our thoughts directly – to communicate to the audience openly, and recover a theatrical language distorted by fifty years of communism. It is not an easy task to achieve, but the fact that so many new dramaturgical voices have arisen in the past few years is reason enough to make us optimistic. Four of the most promising of these Romanian playwrights, young and very young, are present in this collection, each one with a specific way of seeing the Romanian reality, each one with a style of communicating to the audience an articulated artistic vision of the society we are living in. With them lies our hope of forming a credible and consistent playwriting movement that can break through the lethargy and become a driving force in our contemporary Romanian theatre.

This anthology also reinforces a very special connection and friendship, that between Irish and Romanian theatre – two cultural spaces, two societies for which the theatre has played a primordial part, keeping alive the people's hope in times of rough political oppression and grief. There is between the Irish and us this special affinity in art and in feeling, a spiritual liaison, with deep roots in historical and cultural similarities.

This is why the publishing of this volume is a moment of celebration and an open door towards other rewarding collaborations between us.

Editor's Preface

Andrei Marinescu

This anthology is the outcome of several years of collaboration between theatre people in Romania and Ireland. Traditionally much of the energy on the Romanian stage has come from the director's imaginative reinterpretation of the classics, but recently young practitioners have been seeking out new texts to allow a contemporary voice to be a stronger element in the whole creation of theatre. And Ireland is seen as the home of the writer. In the autumn of 2002 we published in Bucharest a collection of contemporary Irish plays in Romanian translations *Patru Piese Despre Noi* (Four Plays About Us). The Act Theatre, which specializes in presenting new work, staged superb rehearsed readings of all four; two of them – Eugene O'Brien's *Eden* and Malachy McKenna's *Tillsonburg* – have since been given a full production by other Romanian companies, and we hope that Conor McPherson's *Port Authority* and Gerald Stembridge's *The Gay Detective* will soon also be staged.

This infusion of energy into Romanian theatre through translations from Ireland and the other important dramaturgies of the world has not been inhibiting but rather stimulating the

Romanian playwriting movement, weakened by years of control and censorship. Now, having seen and absorbed what is going on in the rest of the world, the talented writers in this corner of Europe need to take their place in an international theatrical dialogue.

There have of course been, before but mostly after 1989, many Romanian theatre pieces published in English. But, despite the formal linguistic skills of the Romanian based translators, the intrinsic value of these plays was often lost in English texts that sounded flat, almost insipid. With the idiom and charm of the language of the originals irreparably lost through the act of translation, the plays became all but impossible to stage for an English speaking audience.

This is why I decided that for this anthology we had to develop a fresh concept regarding how these translations should be made. Consulting with Bucharest's Act Theatre and other people committed to the encouragement of new writing, I settled on texts by four of the writers most identified with the new wave – Petre Barbu, Mimi Brănescu, Lia Bugnar and Gianina Cărbunariu. I made literal translations, and then met at the idyllically peaceful Tyrone Guthrie Centre in the centre of Ireland with them and three young Irish playwrights – Michael Collins, Christian O'Reilly and Paul Meade – to work on final versions that would appeal to English-speaking audiences. All of this enterprise was under the guidance and sponsorship of the Stewart Parker Trust which works in Ireland to support emerging playwrights and of the Ireland Romania Cultural Foundation.

The Centre in Annaghmakerrig and its Director Sheila Pratschke nurtured in their very special way this intermingling between the two cultural spaces so far apart geographically but so similar in spirit, and the outcome was new and enduring friendships between people intent on re-shaping theatre in Ireland and Romania.

But the broader purpose of the enterprise is here in this volume, making accessible the Romanian texts to new audiences. We hope that *East of Eden* may create for the reader an eloquent enough image of what playwriting means in Romania at this time and shed some kind of light on the period of 'transition' that Romanian society is now passing through. Transition to what? That seems to be the main question being posed in these texts. We don't know. For the moment we are stuck, East of Eden.

East of Eden: New Romanian Plays

Bones For Otto

By Lia Bugnar

Translated by Andrei Marinescu
Adapted by Michael Collins

17th September 2004

Characters

Woman One
Woman Two
Otto

***Woman One** stands by the side of the road, dressed provocatively but not without taste. Her handbag is slightly oversized. She looks to her left, apparently waiting for something – perhaps a car. The sound of a car approaching. Her head turns, following the car as it passes in front of her at speed. She looks to the right, staring after the car. She adjusts her posture – checking her feet, arching her back, trying to make her breasts look bigger than they actually are. She relaxes and looks to her left again.*

***Woman Two** appears, walking slowly and confidently. She stops at a certain distance from Woman One. She also starts looking to her left. Once in a while, she glares boldly at Woman One, sizing her up. Every now and then Woman One returns her stare.*

The sound of a car approaching. Woman One arches her back. Woman Two gestures for the car to stop. Their heads turn, following the car as it passes in front of them without stopping. Woman Two swears incoherently, more to herself than anyone else. They look to their left again – another car is heard approaching. Woman One arches her back, Woman Two waves, turns around and wiggles her arse. The car doesn't stop. Woman Two swears again, this time more coherently. She looks brazenly at Woman One, as if she's about to say something. Another car is heard approaching. Both of them look to their left again. Woman Two makes a few gestures, even more suggestive than before. Woman One arches her back. The car doesn't stop.

Woman One: (*To Woman Two*) Excuse me. Look, I hope you don't mind me saying … (*Woman Two turns to Woman One*) Wouldn't it be better for both our chances if you crossed to the other side of the road? I mean … You could take all the cars going in that direction …

Woman Two: (*Approaches Woman One and looks across the road to where Woman One is nodding*) Where? On that side?

Woman One: Exactly … And eventuaaaaa – !*Woman Two has grabbed her by the hair and punched her in the stomach.*

Woman Two: Get the fuck out of here, you stupid bitch! (*Walks away from Woman One, who is bent over, clutching her stomach*) What do you think, you own the fucking road!?

Woman One is coughing and holding her stomach. Another car approaches. Woman Two wiggles her arse. The car doesn't stop.

Woman One recovers slightly. She moves away from Woman Two, never taking her eyes off her. Suddenly she changes her mind and goes back towards her. Woman Two gives her a fierce look.

Woman One: I shouldn't have to move. I was here first … (*Woman Two stands, hands on hips, ready to attack. Woman One stops and looks at her*) Yeah! And don't give me that look! I was here first. Not that that's anything worth bragging about! I was told if I got here first, I could hustle no problem. 'Cause the roads are fair game … I mean … first here: it's *their* path … Which is ridiculous anyway. This road doesn't even *have* a path! (*Close to tears*) But look, I will move … *after* you explain why you punched me in the stomach.

Woman Two: (*Amused*) Where did you want me to punch you?

Woman One: Nowhere. That's what I mean. Why go around punching people like that?

Woman Two: (*Looks at her, slightly taken aback. Takes out a knife*) Maybe you'd prefer a taste of this? Listen, if you don't get the fuck outta here fast …

Woman One: (*Stupefied*) You have to be joking with that thing!

Woman Two: (*Comes from behind and holds the knife to her throat*) I'm gonna cut you, bitch! You hear me? Do you? Are you gonna leave or do I have to cut you up?

Woman One: (*More astonished than scared*) I think you're bluffing. This is just a show of bravado!

Woman Two: (*Doesn't understand*) Show of what?

Woman One: Bra … You're pretending. Faking it!

Woman Two is pressing the knife against her neck. Woman One squeals.

Woman Two: How's that feel? How's that for faking it?

Woman One: (*Quietly*) Yes! You're just trying to scare me!

Woman Two: (*Bewildered, lets her go*) You're completely fucked up, girl! Jesus! (*Blesses herself*) What if I'd cut your throat? Holy fuck! Here I am, a knife to her throat and she's … You won't die in your bed, girl, trust me! And for what? You could've gone ten metres down the road … Would that've fucking killed you? 'Just go if that's what she wants … I mean she's got a knife …' You're one stupid bitch!

Woman One is crying.

Woman Two: Are you crying? What're you crying for?

Woman One keeps crying.

Woman Two: Come on, I'm not gonna do anything … Come on, stop crying!

Woman One starts crying even harder. Woman Two looks at her, powerless and sad, every now and then telling her to 'Stop crying'.

Woman One: Please, excuse me! I'll be fine in a minute, I'm sorry!

Woman Two: And stop being so fucking polite!

Woman One: (*Still whining*) I'm not.

Woman Two: Yes, you are. 'Excuse me'. '*Oh*, please, I'm *so sorry*'. What's your problem?

Woman One: It's just my way of speaking …

Another car approaches. Woman One arches her back and wipes mascara from her cheeks. Woman Two wiggles her arse and makes obscene gestures. The car doesn't stop.

Woman Two: (*Shouting after the car*) Hey! Dickhead! (*To Woman One*) How do you like my way of speaking?

Woman One: Are you please going to tell me why you hit me?

Woman Two: I hit you so you wouldn't hit me first.

Woman One: You thought *I* was going to hit *you*?

Woman Two: I thought you'd want to defend your patch. Like any normal whore.

Woman One: Actually, there's probably enough room for both of us. I won't take your clients if you don't take mine.

Woman Two: What planet are you from? Someone stops and picks me up. I'm standing there right beside you. That isn't me taking your client?

Woman One: No!

Woman Two: No?

Woman One: No!

Woman Two: Aren't you the fucking angel? I take the guy and solve his problem for a hundred dollars. Meanwhile, you're just standing there?

Woman One: Is that what you charge? A hundred dollars?

Woman Two: Well … A hundred! I was just talking … What do you care what I charge? What, did I go asking you?

Woman One: Five hundred dollars.

Woman Two: Five hundred?

Woman One: It's a lot, isn't it?

Woman Two: *(Blessing herself)* You must be … some angel, alright.

Woman One: I know it's a lot, but for some people money's just not a problem. It doesn't matter to them.

Woman Two: So they just give it to you?! 'Here, take five hundred. Fuck it, take six! What do I care?' Even the girls in the hotels don't get two hundred!

Woman One: I know. I looked into that. But it's too crowded there. Too difficult to get in.

A car approaches. Woman One arches her back. Woman Two wiggles her arse. The car doesn't stop. They look to the left. Woman Two sneaks a glance at Woman One.

Woman One: *(To self)* Five hundred dollars. Not a penny less.

Woman Two: *(Short pause)* And what exactly do you do to them for five hundred dollars?

Woman One: Do to them?

Woman Two: I mean, what do you do for that kind of money?

Woman One: I don't do anything to them. I offer my body.

Woman Two: *(Looks at her* silently) Look, I think I'll just head up the road here. Not to keep you from all your customers.

Woman One: Ok then. *(Woman Two takes two steps)* Hey …!

Woman Two: Yeah?

Woman One: Good luck!

Woman Two: (*Looking at her, puzzled*) Yeah, whatever …

They move as far away from each other as the stage allows. They exchange glances every now and then. Woman One waves and smiles at Woman Two. Woman Two waves back, slightly embarrassed. The sound of a car. Woman Two gestures. Woman One arches her back. The car doesn't stop.

Woman One: (*After a while*) You want an apple?

Woman Two: No. (*Quietly, after a pause*) Thanks.

Woman One: Chocolate?

Woman Two: No. No thanks.

Woman One approaches Woman Two, while eating an apple.

Woman One: You think it's because it's Monday?

Woman Two: What?

Woman One: Their lack of … sexual appetite.

Woman Two: (*Repeating mechanically*) Their lack of what …? I don't think the day has anything –

Woman One: Then what do you think it is? Why aren't they stopping?

Woman Two: You want to know what I think?

Woman One: Yeah …

Woman Two: I think you're a nutcase, that's what.

Woman One: Pardon?

Woman Two: I don't care that you're a freak … But you're ruining *my* luck too. You're jinxed, that's what. You and your hundreds of dollars! If I get twenty dollars, I kiss the notes and stick them to my forehead! And I promise the guy I'll do it for free the next time he stops! Look, I've nothing against you personally but I want you to stay away from me. Just go somewhere else! Either that or *I'll* go because you're jinxing me too.

Woman One: You stay. I'll go.

Woman One disappears offstage. Woman Two is left alone, tortured by remorse, looking backstage, and grumbling to herself. A car passes but she doesn't do anything. She realizes after it has passed and waves after it. She gives up.

Woman Two: (*To self*) Crying like a child … over nothing. (*Shouts*) Hey, girl! Don't cry! Hey! Come back here, I want to tell you something! (*No answer*) Come on, stop crying! You hear me?! All right. Give me an apple so.

Woman One comes closer and takes an apple from her bag. Woman Two takes it and rubs it on her sweater.

Woman One: … I already cleaned it.

Woman Two: Oh! Thanks.

Woman Two takes a bite of the apple. Woman One looks at her not knowing whether to leave or not. She decides to leave.

Woman Two: Look, I didn't really mean that … That you're jinxed … But it's just you *are* a bit odd. And some people bring bad luck … I mean if you're even near them you might as well go home. It rubs off on you. There's this girl, Flexi … When Flexi shows up they have a whip around. They pay her to go home. It's like she puts a curse on everyone …

Woman One: Her name's Flexi?

Woman Two: It's not her real name. She's nicknamed. (*Thinks for a second and concludes*) That's her nickname.

Woman One: And who's she? Is she a prostitute too?

Woman Two: Not a prostitute. She's a whore.

Woman One: Isn't that the same thing?

Woman Two: Prostitute: that's what they say on the news. Or when they're talking to their wives. I suppose they just don't like how the word 'whore' sounds. They're all just a bunch of perverts anyway. Too scared to pick one up and see for themselves. The girls in the hotels, maybe you could call *them* prostitutes. But down here on the side of the road, we're all just whores. Whores and don't forget it.

Car engine. The moves. It doesn't stop.

Woman One: You know what. I think you might be right … Maybe I am jinxed. If you were on your own, would anyone have stopped by now?

Woman Two: I don't know … Yeah, probably. I'm usually pretty lucky. Two or three quick tricks and I'm gone. I don't need any more than that. God looks after me because I'm not greedy. I don't go around asking for hundreds of dollars like you.

Woman One: You think that's it? That's what's jinxed me?

Woman Two: I don't know what to think. But five hundred dollars. You must be crazy if you think –

Car. The usual routines. It doesn't stop.

Woman Two: Let's eat that chocolate you had. Then I'm going home seen as it's so dead here today.

Woman One takes out the chocolate and a package.

Woman Two: What's that?

Woman One: Bones. For the stray dogs. There's so many of them everywhere and I hate seeing them hungry.

Woman Two: You mean you had lunch out here and you kept the bones?

Woman One: No … I brought them with me from home. Thought I might find some strays here. But there aren't any.

Woman Two: Actually, there are. Flexi says it's *her* dog. 'How can it be yours,' I go, 'if you don't take him home?' But she still reckons it's her guard dog. She thinks it's a pure-bred.

Woman One: What breed is it?

Woman Two: A bit of everything. Some kind of mongrel. But she insists he's a pure-bred. 'What're you doing, Flexi,' I go, 'keeping your pure-bred out on the road like that?' But the funny thing is he actually obeys her! She even gave him a name. (*Short pause*) Hang on, I'll call him. You can give him the bones. Otto! Otto!

Otto appears. Woman One gives him the bones.

Woman One: Otto! He's so cute!

Woman Two: (*Looking at Otto*) He's cute alright! Flexi said she's gonna keep him in the grounds of her villa. And send him to the poshest dog-school to learn all kinds of fancy tricks. Then when she's lounging by the swimming pool he can bring her out the paper.

Woman One: She has a swimming pool?

Woman Two: A swimming pool? She lives in a broken shower! She hasn't a tooth in her head! She was just talking, you know, dreaming …

Woman One: If that's what she wants with all her heart … then some day she will get it.

Woman Two: Of course she wants it … with all her everything! But she won't get it! 'Cause she's jinxed, that's why! I thought we were having that chocolate.

Woman One: Oh! Sure!

Woman One breaks the chocolate in two and gives her one half.

Woman Two: (*Watching Woman One eating*) We can make a hundred dollars together if we do a 'three'.

Woman One: A 'three'?

Woman Two: You know … someone stops, we offer him a 'three'. I mean, you and I kiss or whatever, rub each other … things like that … and the guy watches. A hundred dollars! Fifty for you, fifty for me!

Woman One: I couldn't. I'm not a lesbian.

Woman Two: That's why I suggested it! I wouldn't go kissing you if you were! But seen as we're both straight, it doesn't matter! We kiss, we moan … things like that … Only don't laugh! If you laugh, they think you're making fun of them and they get angry.

Woman One: Fifty dollars … What can I do with that?! I need *five hundred.* (*Very sad*) Today.

Woman Two looks at her for a while.

Woman Two: (*Serious*) You owe money? What, you got a loan and now you have to pay it back?

Woman One: No … I … (*Sighing*) I have to get to New Zealand.

Woman Two: You what?

Woman One: To a contest. I was selected for this contest. I have to be there for the fifteenth. They're paying for everything else. But I have to buy the ticket. (*Voice trembling*) Nearly five hundred dollars!

Woman Two: Don't start that again! You're driving me mad with all this crying! What kind of contest is it? What are you, a runner or something?

Woman One: A singing contest. I'm a singer.

Woman Two: Oh! A singer! A pop-singer.

Woman One: I sing Opera.

Woman Two: (*With pity*) You're an Opera singer.

Woman One: Don't you like opera?

Woman Two: (*Not wanting to hurt her feelings*) I'm sure it's great but all that screaming they do. You should start your own girl-band though! That's where the money is.

Woman One: Now, that's not true!

Woman Two: Don't you read the magazines? They have fancy cars … villas all over the place … you name it …

Woman One: It's not true that they scream! At the opera, I mean … There's no screaming! Just the most wonderful music you ever heard.

Woman Two: Well, on that I can't really argue … 'Cause I've never been to one.

Woman One: That's such a shame. I don't know how people can survive without music. Without *art* ...

Woman Two: Yeah, sure! … (*Looks at her*) You sound like a child! You're talking like my son does!

Woman One: You have a son?

Woman Two: Third class. He's really bright. Top of his class.

Woman One: You're married then?

Woman Two: Divorced. My son's like you … about the art, I mean … He paints!

Woman One: He paints? Is he talented?

Woman Two: Talented? His pictures look like photographs!

Car, the movements, it doesn't stop.

Woman Two: I bought him some *Acrylics* for his birthday. You know how expensive all that stuff is … the paint, the brushes … But I don't mind 'cause he's so careful with them … Looks after them like a grown up would. And he never asks for toys or footballs, any of that … Ever since he was little … 'Lead pencil', 'lead pencil …!'

Woman One: Red pencil?

Woman Two: That's all he's ever been interested in.

Woman One: And the Father? Does he help out with money?

Woman Two: I don't need any help! My son has everything he wants. I even bought him rollerblades! To try and get him outside more. You know, to play with the other kids.

Woman One: And does he come to see him?

Woman Two: Sometimes. He pays maintenance …

Woman One: Why'd he leave?

Woman Two: He didn't leave. I threw him out 'cause he was a whore-chasing bastard. I tried everything to cure him but when a man's a whore-chaser there's just nothing you can do about it. I'm not even mad at him though. It's not his fault. Some men prefer not to know the woman they're sleeping with. He used to say a whore is more honest than a wife. You just give her money and that's it. But with a wife: you give her your soul and it's *still* not enough …

Woman One: And does he know what you do now?

Woman Two: Nobody knows! And even if he did – it was him who gave me the idea. This is a job that never goes out of business … And you're not hurting anyone either … Men who use whores do it because they prefer whores. That's their nature. It's not his fault. It's not the wife's fault. That's just how it is.

Woman One: You ever think of getting remarried?

Woman Two: No way. (*After a pause*) I loved the first guy … too much. That's why I left him, because … well, because I loved him so much. And when I'm with a good-looking guy … as good-looking as he was … What I do, I pretend that it's actually him … and I'm that whore he wants just because he doesn't know her … and I pretend that afterwards he'll come home with me, after he's cheated on me … with me … (*Pause*) I don't care about marriage. And anyway, it's not like there isn't a man in the house. My son is there and he's the spitting image of his Father! Absolute image of him! I just hope he doesn't take after him! But when he puts his hand behind his head like this … and looks at me with one eye half-shut … I can't explain it how alike they are … Still I think he's a better person than his Father. But it freaks me out how alike they are … I wish I could show you this painting he did one time …

Car, movements, nothing.

Woman Two: (*After a pause*) It was of this beautiful house … like in the movies … But not like kids usually draw … more like something a grown up would do! With a door handle, gutters … and a letterbox … (*Her voice is trembling*) even a rubbish bin … And the sun in the sky … with its rays … And in the sun he'd painted my face, smiling. And near it was this cloud, again my face in it but this time sad … And it was covering the sun a bit … With raindrops falling from it … and if you looked closely you could see they were little hearts … And the window of the house was open … Me inside, you could see my back … doing something … but you couldn't make out what … So I asked him, 'What was I doing in there, sweetie?' and he said that … I was making plum tarts. But he'd no room to draw them. 'But why put me in so many places,' I asked him, 'and you're not there with me?' So he said he was there too, but he's in his room painting that exact picture. And that afterwards he was going to eat some of the plum tarts. (*Deep breath*) Look at me, I'm ranting! (*Looks to the left. Takes a few steps away. Comes back again*) I can tell we're not gonna get any business today. It's not your fault … Just some days are like this … We might as well go home!

Woman One: You go. I'll hang on another bit. You never know …

Woman Two: Come on … go home. Things aren't that bad. There'll be other contests … If they picked you this time, you'll get picked for something else again … Who knows what'll happen! Come on, let's go.

Woman One: (*Morose*) I'm giving it another five minutes. (*Passionately*) I can't go yet. You've no idea how hard I worked for this! (*Looks down road*) I'm not moving! (*With hatred*) These perverts! When I get my money I'll go! Not before! (*A car passes*) Pervert! (*After a while*) Poor man! He's probably going home to his wife.

Woman Two: Sing me something … Whatever you're supposed to sing over there … in New Zealand …

Woman One: I thought you didn't like Opera … All that screaming!

Woman Two: But you said they don't scream.

Woman One: I know …

Woman Two: Come on.

Woman One: Well, if you really want me to …

Woman Two: I do. Sing it.

Woman One performs the final aria from La Traviata. Pause. Both are silent. They look to the left. Cars pass but they don't react.

Woman Two: The fuck was that called?

Woman One: La Traviata. It's an aria from La Traviata.

Woman Two: And the woman … Why does she have to die?

Woman One: She's a courtesan … Violetta.

Woman Two: A courtesan?

Woman One: Kind of a whore from the old days. Actually, not *kind* of. She *was* a whore. A proper whore.

Woman Two: Then call her that. If that's what she was.

Woman One: Yeah, well, *this whore* falls in love with a nobleman and … well, she dies because of a lung problem. And he's all heartbroken about it …

Woman Two: You mean … All that beautiful music is about a diseased whore?

Woman One: Something like that. A whore with tuberculosis.

Woman Two: So to sing about a diseased whore you had to become one? Isn't that taking the role a bit too seriously?

Woman One: These last two months, since I was selected, all I've been doing is trying to get my hands on that money. I've tried everything. But nobody'll help me. No one gives a damn whether or not I get to sing La Traviata in New Zealand. And tomorrow I have to pay for the ticket or I lose the booking. So I don't care what I have to do. Even if it means sleeping with some stranger. So long as it gets me what I've spent all this time working so hard for. And this is the chance I've been dreaming of. Better to be fucked for five minutes than fucked for the rest of your life! So come on, pervert! You better stop because I'm ready! Where are you with my money?! (*Looking to left*) Come on, pervert, come and get the most grateful whore you'll ever meet! I'll fuck your brains out!

Car passes. It doesn't stop.

Woman Two: What's he doing? Is he backing up?

Woman One: Yeah … He's waving …

Both looking right with inquiring gestures.

Woman Two: He wants *you.*

Woman One: I don't think so … (*Gestures*) I think he wants both of us! (*Grave*) What'll we do? Should we kiss?

Woman Two: No! No! I'm telling you, it's just you he wants … Go talk to him!

Woman One: I'll go see!

Woman One leaves.

Woman Two: Hey!

Woman One: What?

Woman Two: Get the cash up front. Bring it back here. Cash first.

Woman One: Thanks!

Woman One leaves. Woman Two remains alone, looking after her. A car passes. Woman Two waves but it doesn't stop. Lights down.

Lights up. Woman One comes running back to Woman Two.

Woman One: I got it! I got it! (*Waving money. Both excited*) Can you tell if it's fake?

Woman Two: Show me. (*Examines notes in light*) They look good. (*Delight. Woman One takes the money back and puts it in her bag*) Go on then, he's waiting! And be careful! Watch the money.

Woman One: (*Leaving*) I'm going. I'll be back in a bit! (*Comes back*) Ah! You know what, what if it's a trick and he grabs it back afterwards? You hold it for me! (*Takes out the money. A bone falls from her bag*) What's this? Oh! Take this too. In case Otto comes back.

Woman One runs off. Woman Two stands, money in one hand, bone in the other, looking after Woman One. She looks at the money. Freezes. Licks her finger and starts counting it. Considering. Looks at bone.

Woman Two: (*Calling*) Otto! Otto! (*Otto arrives. She gives him the bone and pets him*) How's the bone? Does Otto like the bone? (*Long pause*) What'll I do with that silly girl's money? (*Short pause*) Ok, I'll count to twenty. If no cars pass, I'll go home.

Otherwise I'll wait for her, the jinxed whore that she is. 1,2,3,4,5,6,7,8,9,10,11,12, 14, 15, 16, 17, 18, 19, 20. Bye, Otto!

Lights down.

Lights up. Stage empty. Woman One enters. She looks around. She can't believe her eyes. She sits on the ground. Woman Two appears. She sits beside her. Silence.

Woman One: You give him the bone?

Woman Two: Mmhm. (*Beat*) Wolfed it down! (*Silence*) Oh! Don't forget this … (*Hands her the money*)

Woman One: (*Holding back the tears*) I thought you were gone.

Woman Two: So did I.

Woman One: Why'd you come back?

Woman Two: I thought about you singing to those New Zealanders about whores who get lung disease from standing on draughty roads. How was it, anyway?

Woman One: I don't know. I suppose … it was ok for the first time.

Woman Two: He any good?

Woman One: You mean the …?

Woman Two: Mmhm.

Woman One: You see, I don't know … I mean, I told him the whole story … the contest, the plane ticket, La Traviata …

Woman Two: And …?

Woman One: So I sang for him. Pretty well … Even better than for you. It was good practice, you know … Like a rehearsal. There was one note that I –

Woman Two: Did he fuck you or not?

Woman One: Well … What you mean by …?

Woman Two: Did he fuck you? Did he have 'sexual intercourse' with you?

Woman One: Not really …

Woman Two: Tell me. Stop messing around!

Woman One: He was a very polite gentleman. He listened to me sing and said I had an exceptional voice.

Woman Two: Then what?

Woman One: And that this country should be proud of me.

Woman Two: And?

Woman One: And that he's proud as a Romanian.

Woman Two: Right!

Woman One: And that it's a shame an artist with my talent should be forced to find such a solution for …

Woman Two: That he was right about. Then what?

Woman One: That he was glad to have had the privilege to be able to stop … To offer his assistance.

Woman Two: Good for him!

Woman One: … And he was glad to have saved me from spoiling myself. That, yes, art *demands* sacrifice but not *this kind* of sacrifice!

Woman Two: In a word, he left you gobsmacked!

Woman One: And at the end he said … that …

Woman Two: That what?

Woman One: (*Deadpan*) That I should let him Eat My Soprano Pussy!

Woman Two: You're joking! And what'd you say?

Woman One: Well, for five hundred dollars what would you've said?

Woman Two: (*Yelling delightedly*) I can't believe it! (*Calming down a bit*) And how was it?

Woman One: …A bit weird …

Woman Two: Tell me again. How much did you say that ticket was? The exact amount.

Woman One: 494 dollars.

Woman Two: Great! With the change you can buy me a beer!

The End

Insomniacs: The Far Side of the Accordion

By Mimi Branescu

Translated by Andrei Marinescu
Adapted by Christian O'Reilly

May 31, 2004

Characters

The Man
The Voice
The Other Man
The Wreck

After midnight. Quiet. **The Man** *enters, looking around for something. He wears an old worn suit. He sits down on the bench and stares up at the Moon, preoccupied by it.* **The Voice** *of an old man is heard from the window of a nearby building.*

The Voice: Betty! Beeeetty! (*Beat*) Betty! Beeetty! (*Beat*) Where are you? Are you asleep? Betty! Beeetty! Will you not come here to me, no? (*Beat*) Betty, for Heaven's sake! Betty!

The Other Man *enters, breathing the fresh air of the night. He is also dressed poorly. He is younger than The Man. He pauses when he notices The Man sitting quietly on the bench looking up at the Moon. The Other Man sits on the other end of the bench and stares at The Man, who continues to stare at The Moon, while being aware that he is being watched. The Other Man struggles to say something, but can't get it out. He edges a little closer to The Man and is about to speak, but The Man, feeling uncomfortable at this attention, speaks first.*

The Man: (*Looking at the Moon*) It's so close tonight.

The Other Man: The Moon? Yeah, looks like it's about to fall.

The Man: No chance. It's very secure.

The Man stares determinedly at the Moon. The Other Man edges closer.

The Other Man: God, imagine if it fell down on top of us!

The Man: Impossible. Great forces hold it in place.

The Other Man: Tell me about it. Gigantic. We couldn't move it an inch if we tried.

The Man turns away slightly and stares doggedly at The Moon.

The Other Man: I'm telling you. They've even done a study on it. I was reading about it in a magazine.

The Man: I don't bother with magazines.

The Other Man: Why?

The Man: They don't interest me.

The Other Man: Oh there's loads of interesting things to be found in magazines, believe me.

The Man: (*Impatient*) Not by me

The Man folds his arms and returns his attention to the Moon.

The Other Man: Too bad. You've no idea what you're missing. I could lend you a few amazing ones. Brilliant articles. Mind blowing. They'd really make you think. Still, they've gone way overboard, these scientists. It used to be next to impossible to discover anything new. Now there's three or four a day.

The Man doesn't react. The Other Man edges closer.

The Other Man: You see, in the old times, you only had one discovery every 70 -100 years. Like that the Earth is round. Fair enough. 100 years later – the electric lightbulb. Today, discovery after discovery, the sky's the limit. You can't keep track of all of them and some … Like why would you need a machine that puts your glasses on your nose? Can you not just use your hands? It's beyond me.

The Man: Haven't you noticed? (*Pointing at the Moon*) It's watching us.

The Other Man: You're right. (*Addressing the Moon*) What is it, dear? Is there something you want to tell us? Looks like it wants to talk to us, doesn't it?

The Man: It *is* talking to us. (*Beat, a little sad*) Only we can't understand what it's saying. We don't know the language.

The Other Man: Yeah but it doesn't have a mouth.

The Man: The problem is that we have one. And that we think it's the only way to communicate.

The Other Man: Yeah, but how else? The mouth is for eating and speaking, isn't it?

The Man: Yeah …

The Other Man: So?

The Man: So it's a prejudice. Have a look! It's turned its back to us.

The Other Man quickly looks at the Moon.

The Other Man: Amazing! How can you tell?

The Man: Practice.

The Other Man nods, impressed.

The Other Man: Do you come here often? I mean I haven't seen you before.

The Man: I like discretion.

The Other Man: Very sensible.

The Man: Thank you.

The Other Man: I come here every night.

The Man: It's leaving.

The Other Man: The moon? It looks perfectly still to me.

The Man: A simple optical illusion. In fact, it's already gone.

The Other Man stares at the Moon, puzzled.

The Other Man: I see … Is this what you do? Study the moon?

The Man: No. It's simply an old passion. Believe me, it's worth it.

The Other Man: Oh I'm sure. Otherwise you wouldn't watch it every night, to see when it leaves. I envy you to be honest.

The Man: You've no reason to. You can watch it yourself, I don't mind. There's plenty of space.

The Other Man: Ah but I don't have the knowledge. I'd just stare at it. I'd hardly understand a thing.

The Man: Neither did I, at the beginning. I sacrificed many years to get this far.

The Other Man: I see.

The Other Man gets to his feet, paces, sits again.

The Other Man: Would you mind if …

The Man: What?

The Other Man: I was thinking …

The Man: What about?

The Other Man turns away, hesitating, but then edges closer.

The Other Man: I'd like to share the secret of my life with you.

The Man: Please do … but isn't it a bit too soon?

The Other Man: I suppose I shouldn't …

The Man: (*Turning to The Other Man*) But now that you've started …

The Other Man turns away.

The Other Man: Maybe you're not interested. You've got better things to be doing than listening to the likes of me.

The Man: You don't really know me. I have a passion for the mysteries of human nature. A real secret would give me a pleasure equal to a first step on the Moon.

The Other Man, greatly flattered, turns to The Man.

The Other Man: Would you like to go to the Moon?

The Man: I was giving an example.

The Other Man: Yeah, but as far as I'm concerned, someone like you deserves to walk on the Moon. If you can't, you know, with all your passion – then who can?

The Man shrugs modestly.

The Other Man: I can feel my courage leaving me.

The Man: Let him go. He'll be back.

The Other Man: Yeah, but maybe not today.

The Man: Never mind, you can tell me another time. I'm in no hurry. We'll meet again, I'm sure. When two people are destined to meet, the world becomes a very small place. Not even the Moon can stop them.

The Other Man: Do you mind me not telling you?

The Man: I'll get over it.

The Other Man: (*Anxious*) I hope you don't feel hurt?

The Man: It wouldn't be the first time.

The Other Man: Oh. I'm sorry to hear that.

The Man: It's all right.

The Other Man: I've let you down, haven't I?

The Man: Disappointment has its own purpose in the shaping of the human soul. It's better to be disappointed by you than to be left indifferent. Perhaps nobody has told you this before, it wouldn't surprise me, but one more disappointment is the same as one less, in the course of a lifetime. And whatever you do, you wouldn't be able to change the precise course of my life.

The Other Man ponders this wisdom with awe.

The Other Man: What are you really doing here?

The Man: I am waiting.

The Other Man: For what?

The Man: A sign.

The Other Man looks around his surroundings.

The Other Man: Am I bothering you?

The Man: On the contrary, you're very pleasant.

The Other Man: I don't want to get on the wrong side of you.

The Man: You haven't.

The Other Man: I don't want you to hate my guts.

The Man: I don't.

The Other Man: I've discovered the HSA.

The Man: The what?

The Other Man: The healing sexual act.

The Man: (*Intrigued*) Really?

The Voice: Betty! Don't you want to come to me? Where are you, Betty? Have you left me all alone? Are you asleep? Beeetty!

Where are you, dear? Please come here. I've got something for you!

They look in the direction of The Voice. They resume more quietly.

The Other Man: All by myself. I was just sitting there quietly when it all came to me. Don't you realize what this means?

The Man: Not exactly.

The Other Man: My life has a purpose now. No one can say that I lived in vain. I can rest in peace.

The Man: Were you restless before?

The Other Man: I couldn't sleep at night. Everyone I knew had accomplished something. Everyone except me and one of my neighbours. Nothing. He's the only one left now, the cheeky bastard …

The Man: Cheekiness is a state of mind frequently used in the history of humanity. But be warned, in most cases it is caused by impotence. Impotence, combined with a nature that is willing to succeed at any cost, can turn people into monsters.

The Other Man: (*Puzzled*) You seem to know what you're talking about.

The Man: (*Shrugs modestly*) You were saying something about your neighbour …

The Other Man: Well … He's forty and he hasn't achieved anything yet. I don't know how he sleeps at night. He finally paints his apartment after seven years … so what? He has two stupid kids … what's so amazing about that? His wife's not bad, but what's that got to do with him? He just got lucky, that's all. And listen to this, right. He does nothing at night, absolutely nothing, he doesn't even watch TV. I should know, I'm the one that disconnected his cable. I really don't understand his mentality. Every afternoon I break the lift, so he has to use the stairs when he gets home from work. He comes loaded with bags and stuff every day. All sorts of stupid things. Once he had to carry the TV set up the stairs. Eight floors. (*A proud smile*) All thanks to me. He kept cursing all the way up. I almost died laughing. I had nothing against him, you understand. He started it, honestly. Anyway, why would I lie to you? We've only just met.

The Man: Who knows? Are you sure you're really talking to me right now?

The Other Man: What do you mean? I'm sure of it. At least I think I am. But don't get me wrong, I know you've got better things to be doing.

The Man: Do you really know me?

The Other Man: No. No, I don't. I've never seen you before.

The Man: Than how can you say that you're talking to me if you don't know me?

The Other Man: I never really thought about that. Now that you mention it.

The Man: Well … Anyway, please go on.

The Other Man: Well, he used to give me this look … Full of pity and contempt. Every time I met him I'd ask 'and how are you today, sir?' Never addressed him without calling him 'sir'. I was genuinely happy to see him. Always talked to him very politely. I've never met a more despicable man in my life. I kept trying to help him. Telling him what was new in the building … When the water was going to be cut off, when the electricity bills were going to arrive, when the residents' committee were having their meetings … What they talked about at the meetings. I had a drawer full of every single notice they ever put on the door of that building. Never missed one. Four years and not one of them was hanging on that door more than two minutes before I had it in my hands and shoved it under his door. Do you see what I mean? I did everything for him.

The Man nods sympathetically.

The Other Man: I really liked the poor bastard. I used to watch him leave in the morning and come home in the evening. At the start, he was very pleasant, very polite. He used to hold the door of the lift for me. We went up and down together in that lift 1482 times. I closed and opened the door 1479 times. He only did it three times. 640 times he just stared at me. 480 times he shook my hand. He coughed … (*Taking out and checking his notebook*) 53 times. He sneezed 10 times and I told him 'bless you!' 30 times. He told me the time five times. He asked me how I was twice and once, just once – God it was something else – he said he was really happy to see me!

The Man: Really?

The Other Man: (*Becoming excited at the memory*) I couldn't sleep after that. I was knocking on their door every fifteen minutes. You know, like to give them the news or –

The Man: Them?

The Other Man: Yeah. The wife and kids were there too. I had to keep them up to date, you see, on account of their TV being no good to them.

The Man: Of course.

The Other Man: There was this match on – I forget who was playing, but it was brilliant. Seven or eight goals – imagine. Then more news, then a movie, then the night news. Then another movie – that one was a bit dirty, though. I made sure to keep the dirty stuff out of the story – you know, because of the children.

The Man nods in agreement.

The Other Man: They must have fallen asleep at some point. Or else the bell broke, 'cos they stopped answering the door. I really missed them 'til morning. I couldn't sleep, so I made them some pancakes. Then I cleaned the flat a bit, did some vacuuming. I really got loads done in those few hours, while they were sleeping. You should have seen the look of surprise on their faces when they saw me in the morning, with this massive plate of hot pancakes for them. They just couldn't believe their eyes. I outdid myself that night.

The Man: Did they eat the pancakes?

The Other Man: Not nearly as enthusiastically as I expected. In fact, I had to eat the last six myself. Had to gobble them down, standing there in their doorway. They were in a hurry to get to work.

The Man: You didn't know what time they were supposed to go to work?

The Other Man: Of course I did.

The Man: Then you should have got there earlier.

The Man: I know, but I thought they could've at least stayed a bit longer, for the pancakes' sake. I mean it's not every day you get pancakes at five in the morning, is it?

The Man: You have a point.

The Other Man: Then, out of the blue, he stopped saying 'hello' to me.

The Man: Why?

The Other Man: (*Shrugs. Pause*) I was trying to get hold of him, but they must have gone away somewhere. I thought I heard running water when I was listening at their door. The last thing they needed was to be flooded. It was a good thing I had the keys to all the apartments in the building … Got them cut myself, you never know when they might come in handy. A fire, a disaster …Anything can happen.

The Man: God forbid!

The Other Man: When I opened that door and had a good look around … It was the first time I really felt let down by him... The state of the place … Such chaos … Such bad taste … A blue toilet seat? I felt like throwing it out the window. And blue walls? I had to force myself not to scrape the paint off. Could have done it in only half an hour. But in the end I just had to do something to help him. I just couldn't resist. So I did some small things – nothing major. What could I do? We're human beings not animals …

The Man nods approvingly.

The Other Man: I put the bed where the wardrobe was and I moved the wardrobe into the bed's place. Straight away the room started coming to life. So I pushed the fridge into the hallway and I carried the TV into the kitchen. I was in the middle of cleaning the windows when he arrived. 'Welcome, neighbour,' I said to him. 'I've made a few changes here, had to be done, there was no other way … I'll finish the windows in a second.'

Pause. The Man looks at him expectantly, with hope. The Other Man looks bitterly disappointed.

The Other Man: He didn't say a word, just gave me this look.

The Man shakes his head.

The Other Man: A simple 'thanks' would have been enough. That's all I needed. After all the help I'd given him, without even being asked. (*Pause*) Maybe he was put out 'cos I'd stopped calling him 'sir', maybe he thought I was being too familiar, I dunno. (*Pause*) I just walked out …

The Man: What a man …

The Other Man shrugs.

The Man: A dog, not a man! You should have given him a few slaps.

The Other Man: You think it didn't cross my mind? I decided he wasn't worth it. I just gave him a dirty look, after he shut the door. Then I left.

The Man: Good for you. (*Pause*) And in a civilized country you'd have been paid for all your work …

The Other Man: No, that would have been the last straw – if he'd thrown money at me, you know what I mean? To be honest he did put his hands in his pockets when he saw me – I almost turned purple with shame, but he kept them in 'til I got out of the house. He only took them out to close the door behind me.

The Man: What a thug!

The Other Man: As if I needed his money!

The Man: Awful.

The Other Man: That's why I'm so glad I discovered the healing sexual act. And that I discovered it before he did. Otherwise, it would have been worthless. I showed him.

The Man: You sure did. I bet he's sorry now.

The Other Man: He'll never know. I'd rather take my secret to the grave than let him hear one single word of it. Let him die ignorant if he doesn't know to appreciate people.

The Man: No, if he's stupid, let him live. The longer the better.

The Other Man: I even changed his doormat – you know, as a favour. I bought some paint to freshen up his door. I'd rather drink that paint now.

The Man: I don't think that would be such a good idea. It's no good for you. Destroys your stomach. It has all kinds of chemicals in it.

The Other Man: Really?

The Man: I drank a small glass of ink once and I didn't feel too well after it … Paint is even worse. Was it the thick kind?

The Other Man: Like yoghurt.

The Man: Oh that stuff would kill you.

The Other Man: So what? You call this living? Every time I think about it I feel like crying. And his wife had such beautiful hair. God, she cost me a fortune.

The Man: How?

The Other Man: She changed her hair colour every two weeks.

The Man: (*Puzzled*) You were paying for that?

The Other Man: No, I was betting against the other neighbours. Red came after blonde. Green after red. Then black after green. And then blonde again. Blue. Green. Red again. I was going mad. Once she used six different shades of red, one after the other. Then, bam, all of a sudden, metal grey. There was no way you could predict that. Impossible. (*Pause*) The secretary of the residents association was such a jammy bastard.

The Man: Why?

The Other Man: He was following her. He got friendly with the hairdresser. So friendly that they had a baby. He practically furnished his house with our money. That hair-dying cow got rich on us too.

The Man: He's not worth getting upset about.

The Other Man: To hell with the old fart. He's just a crook.

The Man: I wasn't talking about the secretary. I mean the neighbour. Forget about him. I've had to let go so many times, to get over things. Tell yourself, 'forget it, he'll get his comeuppance in the end'. It's not for us to judge.

The Other Man: Judging him wouldn't change a thing.

The Man: It could give you temporary relief, but –

The Other Man: No, it wouldn't do me any good. What kind of judgement does he deserve? No judgement would be enough for him. You'd feel like grabbing him and throwing him into a corner, away from anyone else. It's not fair.

The Man: God sees everything.

The Other Man: Yeah, right. These fellas can dodge God when they put their mind to it.

The Man: I don't think so.

The Other Man: How do you mean?

The Man: I'm telling you.

The Other Man looks at The Man with awe.

The Other Man: Really?

The Man: You don't want to know.

The Other Man: Come on …

The Man: What? You think I'm joking? …

The Other Man: No, God no. You're a very serious person. Anyone with an ounce of sense could see that.

The Man: So many times I've had to draw the line and say … Thank God I know how to stand erect. To follow my path, not to be bothered with rubbish. And I've had to deal with all kinds of idiots, believe me. I know my way. Otherwise I'd have ended up like you.

The Other Man: What do you mean like me?

The Man: Unhappy.

The Other Man: You don't know what you're saying, mister. You don't know me. I'm perfectly happy. Now that I've discovered the HSA, I've no reason to be unhappy. It wasn't easy, I'll give you that, but things are different now. Other people chase happiness now, not me, no siree. (*Pause*) Such a big deal over … happiness … horse manure, load of shite.

The Man: I don't know …

The Other Man: You think I'm talking crap?

The Man: I don't know.

The Other Man: Can't you understand that I'm happy? Even too happy.

The Man: Share it with other people then.

The Other Man: Sure, if they know how to behave properly. (*Pause*) I'd be glad to. But I'd have to be convinced that they need it.

The Man: They all need it. (*Pause*) But only the wise ones have it.

The Other Man smiles, delighted at this compliment, and immediately forgets his anger. There is a happy, self-satisfied pause between them. The Man then removes his shoes, and stretches his feet, wriggling his toes. There are holes in the base of his socks. The Other Man observes this anxiously, wanting to do the same. The Man notices this and gestures for The Other Man to join him in this pleasure. The Other Man, delighted, removes his shoes, imitating the pleasurable gestures of The Man. But The Other Man only has one sock and when The Man is looking away, The Other Man looks enviously at The Man's two socks, unaware that they have holes.

The Other Man: (*Feeling aggrieved*) What about masochists?

The Man: What about them?

The Other Man: They don't need to be happy. They only need to suffer.

The Man: Yes, but they're only happy when they suffer.

The Other Man: Bloody happiness.

The Man: And sadists?

The Other Man: What about them?

The Man: They need to cause suffering in order to be happy.

The Other Man: Like that patronizing gobshite – leaving me with all that paint and keeping his door in that state.

The Man: That's totally different. You know, he might not be as stupid as you think.

The Other Man: He's more nasty than stupid.

The Man: (*With regret for his own situation*) If he was stupid, he wouldn't have a wife and two kids.

The Other Man: Didn't I tell you that his children are idiots too?

The Man: Unless they're not his. Maybe he's just raising them.

The Other Man: Do you think so? I didn't think of that ...

The Man: Maybe she's just staying with him because it suits her ...

Pause.

The Man: Maybe she's not in love with him?

The Other Man ponders this with just a hint of hope. But he sinks quickly into depression.

The Other Man: Oh who cares anyway?

The Man sees that The Other Man finds this subject painful.

The Man: (*Deliberately changing the subject*) He must be making a fortune.

The Other Man: Him?

The Man: Only fools make money these days. Look around you.

The Other Man: He should have painted that door if he was making a fortune rather than making my life miserable.

The Man: Looks can be deceiving.

The Other Man: I lost the best years of my life to make a man of him. And did he even care? No, siree, he didn't. And all the weight I lost because of him, if he only knew … Do you think I always looked like this?

The Man: Losing weight is good. Fat people take up too much space. They eat too much. They drink too much. They're exhausting all our natural resources.

The Other Man: (*Puzzled*) Natural resources? (*Indignant*) I don't eat turf. I don't drink oil either.

The Man: You've no idea what they put in food. Don't ask me, I have no idea either. But you can be sure there's something fishy about it. Did you know that you make a squeaky sound when you chew?

The Other Man: What? Chewing turf?

The Man: Bread, cheese, fish. Whatever you put in your mouth – it doesn't make any difference.

The Other Man: I didn't notice, but I don't brush my teeth very often. Maybe it's because of that? Show me your teeth. (*The Man shows his teeth. They are filthy*) Of course, I see. Yours squeak even when you smile. Squeaky clean. You don't even need to chew.

The Man: It's all toxic, my friend. Full of chemicals. Who can say how many elements in Mendeleev's Table you have already eaten by now?

The Other Man: Really!?! Maybe I've had a few now and then, at special occasions, but I doubt it. Anyway, I've hardly been out since my revelation.

The Man: What revelation – oh this healing act of yours?

The Other Man: The healing sexual act.

The Man: How does it work?

The Other Man: It's not simple. The good thing is it doesn't need any fuel. So there's no consumption.

The Man: Very impressive.

The Other Man: And it's free. You can practice it all by yourself. You don't need any help. It's pretty complicated but you get used to it after a while.

The Man: If it was simple, it would have been discovered by someone else by now.

The Other Man: I don't give a shit about anyone else. As long as he didn't discover it before me. But I don't think he did. Anyway, even if he wanted to discover it now he'd be too late.

The Man: Why?

The Other Man: I complicated it a bit after I discovered it, so that no one could discover it after me.

The Man: Good thinking.

The Other Man: I had to. After all I'd been through before the final revelation … It was really getting to me that I'd never discovered anything. I was getting desperate. Night after night I'd been revisiting my life to see what went wrong. I was the first born child in my family. That should have given me some advantage. Everything was there for me, but nothing … I felt so overwhelmed with resignation. The bags under my eyes almost touched my nose. I couldn't sleep at night. I'd drink three or four cups of coffee to stay awake. The night is the best time for revelations.

The Man: Midnight …

The Other Man: No, later. Closer to the morning, that's when anything seems possible. I was so close a few times, but it just slipped through my fingers.

The Man: How?

The Other Man: I'd be sitting there, stiff as a board, my mind would be getting clearer and clearer. I'd be just about to grab the pen and write everything down – and bang, I'd fall asleep. Just like in that story with the apples and the dragon who kept eating them, the bastard.

The Man: The prince and the golden apples.

The Other Man: That one. The dragon prince. The fella who was stealing the apples.

The Man: No. The dragon was the dragon and the prince was the prince.

The Other Man: What prince?

The Man: The king's youngest son. With the white horse …

The Other Man: What horse?

The Man: Snow-white. The horse that ate fire …

The Other Man: No, he ate apples.

The Man: The prince ate the apples. The horse ate fire. So that he could fly.

The Other Man: The horse could fly?

The Man: To catch the dragon. How else?

The Other Man: I thought the dragon ate the apples?

The Man: Yes he did. And then he flew away …

The Other Man: Riding the horse that ate fire. Now I get it.

The Man: No, without the horse. The dragon flies without a horse. That's why he's a dragon.

The Other Man: Why does he need a horse then?

The Man: Who?

The Other Man: The dragon. Weren't you talking about the dragon?

The Man: Yes I was. But the prince had a horse, not the dragon.

The Other Man: That means that this horse, the white horse, ate the apples.

The Man: No, Snow-White ate fire so that he could fly, with the prince on his back, chasing the dragon, to get the apples back from him.

Pause.

The Other Man: I think I remember. But I thought that the horse's name was Black Beauty, not Snow-White?

The Man: No, Black Beauty was black, that's a totally different story.

The Other Man: He wasn't a horse?

The Man: Yes he was. Only he was black.

The Other Man: I get it. Snow White was a different horse.

The Man: Yes. Snow White isn't Black Beauty. His name is different, isn't it? And Black Beauty doesn't eat fire. He doesn't fly either.

The Other Man: Then what kind of a horse is he?

The Man: An ordinary horse. A race horse.

The Other Man: He must have felt very embarrassed that he couldn't fly. And that he couldn't eat fire. What kind of life did he have?

The Man: Who?

The Other Man: This horse, what's his name? Black Beauty. I feel sorry for him.

The Man: But he had no reason to fly. And he died ages ago anyway.

The Other Man: Good for him. So he doesn't have to eat fire anymore. I can't imagine that eating fire is much fun. You'd damage your throat. And you'd need to carry a bucket of water with you all the time.

The Man: What for?

The Other Man: To put out the fire. You'd burn otherwise.

The Man: It's not the same with horses. They're different. Horses are horses – people are people.

The Other Man: Horses are not people. (*Pause*) I've never thought of it like that.

The Man: They can't be. If they were people you'd call them that – people. If they're called horses, then that's what they are – horses. There's a reason they're called that.

The Other Man: Now I get it. (*Pause*) Where were we?

Pause. They struggle to remember.

The Man: Coffee …?

The Other Man: (*Pause*) Yes. Yes sure.

Pause. The Man is confused.

The Man: No, where you were.

The Other Man: Where I was?

The Man: You were talking about coffee.

The Other Man: Oh. (*Disappointed*) Yes. (*Pause. Fondly*) Ah, coffee.

The Man: (*Aching for it*) Coffee …

The Other Man: I was so close that I couldn't afford to sleep at night anymore. I began to call people. I started with scientists. To see how they discovered things. I made one of them burst into tears. He made me so angry. Just after midnight and he was already in bed. You lazy bastard, I screamed down the phone, have you no decency? Where's this debauchery going to lead you? The world is boiling out there and you, what are you doing about it? … I kept calling him every ten minutes. I even made a homework schedule for him. What a dosser …

The Man: I remember someone calling me.

The Other Man: What time was it?

The Man: Four o'clock in the morning …

The Other Man: What did he want from you?

The Man: He kept asking me if I was sleeping.

The Other Man: And what else?

The Man: What kind of man I was. How I could sleep when the world was boiling …

The Other Man: And what did you tell him?

The Man: That I don't give a toss about the world at four o'clock in the morning. And that my work is my business, thank you very much.

The Other Man: And what did he say?

The Man: He kept screaming at me, calling me 'the antichrist', saying that my only purpose was to destroy the world … That I hadn't discovered my vocation yet. And that I should be very afraid.

The Other Man: When did this happen exactly?

The Man: About two years ago. And there was something else … He said that my voice was so calm that I was obviously possessed. He recommended surgery to have the evil removed.

The Other Man: You have to feel sorry for the guy. I mean he couldn't sleep.

The Man: Maybe he was drinking too much coffee …

The Other Man: Who knows …

The Other Man looks away, embarrassed.

The Man: But he got me thinking that maybe I did need to get checked out. Everybody laughed at me at the hospital, even the doctors. Go home, they said, spare us this rubbish. I had gone there, expecting to stay for a while, I even had my pyjamas with me. I was convinced I was ill.

The Other Man: Maybe the man who called you made a mistake. It's not easy to make a make a diagnosis over the phone.

The Man: But two years ago I had my first revelation.

The Other Man: So the phone call helped you?

The Man: I couldn't sleep afterwards. That's when I started to think about all sorts of things.

The Other Man: Anything interesting?

The Man: Not at first. But after a while, when I got used to staying awake at night, I started to enjoy it. I was waiting for the phone to ring. I couldn't go to sleep without spending an hour or two discussing some vital things with this other guy. Then, when we were just about to become really good friends, he vanished. As if he knew … I had dozens of notebooks full of theories, each one more important than the next. And, little by little, I managed to put it all together.

The Other Man: All by yourself?

The Man: What choice did I have? What a busy time! I began to understand one thing that still makes me shudder. Do you promise not to tell anyone?

The Other Man: I swear.

The Man: Not even the Americans?

The Other Man: Ok.

The Man: Even if they gave you loads of money?

The Other Man: I don't care about money.

The Man: How about 10,000 dollars?

The Other Man: Let's get there first and then we'll see.

The Man: For 10,000 dollars I'd give out any secret.

The Other Man: Then I'll keep it for you. Good enough? …

The Man: (*Momentously*) I am an alien.

Pause.

The Other Man: You're a what?

The Man: I won't say it again.

The Other Man: Like a Martian?

The Man: No … *Another* planet. That's all I can tell you.

Pause.

The Other Man: I see. You look like a normal man, but there is something about you, I can't put my finger on it.

The Man: That's what I'm talking about. Would you have known that I was an alien if I hadn't told you?

The Other Man: It would never have crossed my mind.

The Man: It's not easy for me to hide my true identity. Though at the start I got so good at it that I almost forgot I was an alien. Now I've got the balance right. Every morning I tell myself that I'm a man, I'm a man, I'm a man, so that I won't get found out, but deep down I know my true nature … Of course, we'll keep this between us …

The Other Man: Oh I'll take it to my grave.

The Man: I've been like this since the age of twelve.

The Other Man: Did you spend your childhood among people?

The Man: I don't know. My Mother and Father never said a word. I don't have any brothers or sisters … And I didn't talk to relatives very often. I had to figure it out all by myself.

The Other Man: God love you.

The Man: Are you feeling sorry for me? I can't stand pity. It was given to me, I have to carry my cross … Do you think I don't want to lead a normal life? To go to work, to watch TV.

The Other Man: You're not allowed to watch TV?

The Man: Nobody said so, not in so many words. But I'm not going to take the chance.

The Other Man: You're right. Good thinking. You can't be too careful. You don't want to get yourself fined …

The Man: Who cares about fines? You just pay the fine and that's it … I've got more important things to worry about.

The Other Man: Of course.

The Man: (*Becoming introspective*) I'm talking life and death here … It's no joke. (*Pause, brightening*) Still, when you think about it, aliens die harder …

The Other Man: But they still die in the end.

The Man: We'll see about that.

The Other Man: So, what do you do? … As an alien, I mean? …

The Man: I sharpen razorblades. I have a tool that I carry with me all the time. As soon as I get the feeling that someone suspects I'm an alien, I take out the tool and I start to work on a razorblade. To hide my real identity. So during the day, I act like a normal person. When the night comes, things are different.

The Other Man: You lead a double life. I've heard about people like you.

The Man: Here, I have it with me. (*He takes out the tool*) This is where you put the blade. If you look at me and I sense you're suspicious – bam, I take the tool out. And I start to sharpen. Now you can't tell …

The Other Man: No.

The Man: You see? And I know all the secrets. I have detailed notes about mankind. Books, tapes, photographs, everything …

The Other Man: Who would have thought …

The Man: Ancient Rome, China, Greece, The Ottoman Empire …

The Other Man: I have a map of Romania before the Second World War.

The Man: I have two maps of Ancient Romania.

The Other Man: I have a map of Hungary.

The Man: Who cares about Hungary? (*With pride*) I'm a Romanian alien, not a Hungarian alien. (*Pause*) I have everything, don't you get it!

The Other Man: And what do you do with them?

The Man: What do I do with what?

The Other Man: The maps.

The Man: (*Enigmatic*) I sell them.

The Other Man: To whom?

The Man: To them. When they come to pick me up.

The Other Man: You're an alien spy?

The Man: What else? Was I supposed to just sit, doing nothing? Without a purpose?

The Other Man: When do they come for you?

The Man: That's not a problem. They let me know.

The Other Man: You shouldn't have told me about all this. Now I'm scared.

The Man: You have no reason to be. As long as you're with me you'll be fine.

The Other Man: What if they come after me and torture me for secrets?

The Man: They're friendly. They're civilized.

The Other Man: Yeah, right … I bet they'd stick all kinds of things up my hole.

The Man: Mind your language. Please!

The Other Man: Sorry. My mistake … I have nothing against extraterrestrial civilizations, you know … I've seen all the films. I really like the Spielberg ones. I know more than you think, you know.

The Man: Forget everything.

The Other Man: But why?

The Man: I'll give you a piece of advice. But forget it quickly.

The Other Man: I already have …

The Man: Not so fast! Wait until I tell you …

The Other Man: Okay … So …?

The Man: Spielberg …

Pause.

The Other Man: An alien?

The Man: Quiet! There are many of us. And everywhere.

The Other Man: I thought so.

The Man: My wife never knew.

The Other Man: Was she not one too?

The Man: She was narrow-minded. I tried to interest her. But she slept all the time. I tried to tell her about the tragic situation of human kind. Once I even told her that the only way forward is interstellar partnership, that our future is in the hands of the entire galaxy.

The Other Man: Maybe it was too much for her?

The Man: With an issue like this, of life and death, there's no room for subtleties … You have to speak the truth, loud and clear, and to hell with the consequences …

The Other Man: Like you did with me. But I'm a man …

The Man: That's irrelevant. But if you think about it, men die first anyway. And women …

The Other Man: They die harder.

The Man: Because they put less soul into everything. They don't bother. We're consumed by many things. We're more vulnerable because we're more implicated. That's why we don't sleep …

The Other Man: Sometimes we do …

The Man: During the day, not at night! Now and then. Not like them – every time you look for a woman, she's asleep.

The Other Man: You're right there.

The Man: Other civilizations are looking for us, but we're asleep. They need a sign. So that they know we're open … We can't delay our participation any longer. It takes two to tango.

The Other Man: Two, that's all. If there are three, you can be sure one of them's a thief. I'm speaking from experience, let me tell you. When I was in school, I soon learnt that groups with more than two people are destined to end in tragedy. Like a couple – a 'he' and a 'she' are more than enough. As soon as another 'he' or 'she' enters the equation, everything goes down the tubes.

The Man: I was referring to something else. Something more important.

The Other Man: You didn't let me finish … After I did my military training – it took a bit longer, I was in the navy – I came back home. I admit it, I didn't have the chance to fight in a World War. Not even a Civil War or a local war. What am I saying, I've never even been involved in a decent bar fight …

The Man: You didn't understand what I was saying –

The Other Man: Let me finish … After military service, I came back home. I had to earn a living somehow, but I hadn't a clue what to do. So I was chatting to a neighbour. He said we should go into business as scrap-collectors. I thought why not, I might enjoy it. It seemed like a good idea, even for a guy who hadn't done his military service. God, when I think of the kind of company I used to keep.

The Man: I never did my military service.

The Other Man: That's different. Why would an alien need to do military service?

The Man: But I wanted to do it. I was very hurt when they turned me down.

The Other Man: Why?

The Man: Why …?

The Other Man: I can see why you were hurt, but why did they turn you down?

The Man: Why do you think? A plot. They were afraid that I'd uncover their secrets. They couldn't fool me. 'Not suitable' …

Me?! … Come on! It doesn't matter now anyway. I know everything about them. Uniforms, weapons, strategies … I could be very dangerous.

The Other Man: My partner and I didn't know where to find scrap metal. But then we met a gypsy who had a horse and cart. He told us about places he knew, far away, in fields, that were full of the stuff …The plan was we'd go from village to village and collect the iron … We were going to become rich.

The Man: And?

The Other Man: Well, we went to this village to collect the scrap – there was loads of it. We loaded it into the cart – I had to pay for it all, of course, because the business was my neighbour's idea, the gypsy was providing the cart and so I had to make my contribution. I wouldn't mind, but I'd invested all my savings in the business, I was so excited about it, and the gypsy had convinced me he needed all of it to secure the scrap. Anyway, he tells us to jump off the cart because it's too heavy. And then he said that he'd go ahead and wait for us in the next village, because it was too hot in the sun and the horses would go crazy … We sort of thought there was something fishy about the whole thing, me and my partner, but we didn't complain because of all the money we were going to make.

The Man: And?

The Other Man: He left us in the middle of those deserted fields, without a drop of water. We wandered around like lunatics for two days. We couldn't believe it – the gypsy had fucked off with all our scrap.

The Man: What did you do?

The Other Man: When we finally got to the next village, we went looking for the bastard. But the villagers looked … you know … kind of unfriendly. They left us alone after we bought a few pounds of rotten fish from them. Everyone sells fish in those parts … And we were looking for iron … Jesus! When we finally got home, my partner almost died.

The Man: Why? Had he spent too much time in the sun?

The Other Man: The gypsy had taken his wife.

The Man: To sell her as old iron?

The Other Man: I wouldn't put anything past that fella.

The Man: And?

The Other Man: What?

The Man: Why did you tell me all this? What was your point?

The Other Man: (*Puzzled*) Shall I tell it again?

The Man: No, but what's it got to do with anything?

The Other Man: Don't you get it? If there are three people everything goes wrong.

The Man: (*Puzzled*) But there were four of you?

The Other Man: Oh, including the wife? But the third one brought the fourth person into the equation. Don't you see?

The Man: (*Puzzled*) The point is you can't be financially successful and have a decent marriage as well. It's either one or the other.

The Other Man: I'm not married and my financial situation is quite unstable.

The Man: Either way it's bad.

The Other Man: No doubt about it. It's pretty bad.

Long pause. Now that this latest flight of fancy has come to an end, the reality of their desperate situation is upon them again. They look at their shoeless feet, now a painful reminder of their true selves. The Man quickly puts on his shoes again. The Other Man gratefully does the same.

The Man: (*Very sincere*) The question is – what shall we do?

The Other Man: Let's wait.

The Man: Wait for what?

The Other Man: Wait for the situation to clear up a bit … To see what comes out in the wash. Then we can decide.

The Man: Or shall we just run away?

The Other Man: Now that I think about it, that would be my first choice.

The Man: I can't believe it … We've been talking for such a long time … I was starting to feel that I'd known you for ages and you betray me. You want to run away?

The Other Man: No, only because I used to be a good athlete when I was in school. That's why I told you that we should run away. I'd like to meet the guy who could out-run me. It would have to be for a good cause, of course.

The Man: I can't run any more.

The Other Man: Were you never into sports?

The Man: Chess. But that's a bit static. And I don't like sport anyway. It's a waste of time. But that's not why I don't run.

The Other Man: Why then?

The Man: I had a dream once that someone had tied up my legs. He tied them up in a big red bow and then hung me from a palm tree.

The Other Man: Where?

The Man: (*Reliving the story*) In the desert. And a group of ugly children with skinny legs who were covered in feathers were throwing rocks at me. Then it started to snow. And suddenly, an Eskimo jumped at me holding a big knife in his hand.

The Other Man: In the desert?

The Man: I was surprised too. He was very well dressed and kept rubbing his hands to keep them warm.

The Other Man: I've never heard of such a thing.

The Man: Anything can happen in a dream. He was mumbling something and nodding his head. I realized that he wanted to eat me – his eyes were shining and he was licking his lips. He started to cut small slices of flesh from my body and eat them. Then another Eskimo appeared, even more annoyed than the first one and killed him.

The Other Man: Still in the desert?

The Man: Yes. Then he started to tear chunks of his flesh and eat them.

The Other Man: Whose flesh?

The Man: The first Eskimo's. He was chewing and glaring at me. Then, from time to time, he'd take a bite out of me. But I don't think the second Eskimo liked the way I tasted. He kept making these funny faces, as if he was eating sour grapes. In the meantime, one of my nails kept growing and growing, up into the sky … I don't know where it was growing from, because I had no fingers left. And then a deer with the head of a wolf grew on this nail. When he got near me he started to kick me. He really scared me. Me … Whatever was left of me. Meanwhile, behind him, another deer appeared running down the nail, holding a mini-dish between his horns. And when he opened his mouth, I saw two dwarves having sex. Two male dwarves. One of them noticed me and waved his hand as if to invite me in. One of his teeth was missing and he was holding a gun. He made it quite clear that I was next!

The Other Man: What did you do?

The Man: I turned away. What do you think I did?

The Other Man: And the deer?

The Man: He was gone.

The Other Man: And the dwarves?

The Man: I've always wondered what happened to them. I kept thinking of them for days afterwards. I have no idea.

The Other Man: The deer must have eaten them.

The Man: Which one?

The Other Man: The one with the mini-dish. A deer with a mini-dish would be more informed that an ordinary deer, wouldn't it? And that would make him more dangerous.

The Man: Maybe. After three days I finally woke up. I haven't had another dream since.

The Other Man: No wonder, there was nothing left to dream about. You saw everything that night.

The Man: (*Troubled*) I can still see that little guy with the gun.

Pause.

The Other Man: You should have looked him in the eyes and told him – up yours! I had the same kind of trouble with this fella once. He was coming at me, you know? So I let him get close to me. And when he was just about to grab my neck and strangle me I screamed – what the fuck is your problem? His hands shot up into the air and he froze. And then I ran like hell. It was the best run of my life. Pity I wasn't competing for something. I run really well in real life. (*Beat*) I bet I'd run even better in dreams.

The Man: (*Jealous*) Running is for rabbits.

The Other Man: You couldn't run because you were hanging from a tree with your legs in a bow. (*Hurt*) Antelopes run too, don't they? Even lions run.

The Man: Lions run after antelopes. To eat them.

The Other Man: (*Defensively*) They also run when they're scared. Like when they're being chased by elephants.

The Man: Maybe … but slower.

The Other Man: Of course. Elephants aren't carnivores. They just need to scare lions away sometimes.

The Man: Or maybe they're just playing. Lions are very playful.

The Other Man: I wouldn't play with a lion.

The Men turn away from each other, sulking.

The Man: (*Pause*) Come here. Come closer.

The Other Man: Why?

The Man: I want to tell you something.

The Other Man: So what's stopping you?

The Man: It's important. It regards you personally.

The Other Man: Me?

The Man: That's what I said. I'm serious. Are you going to move closer or not?

The Other Man: Well, I suppose if I have to.

The Other Man moves closer.

The Man: Now take a few steps back.

The Other Man: Did I come too close?

The Man: You're beginning to try my patience now. You don't have to if you don't want to.

The Other Man: Here, here! Is this ok?

The Man: Now take three steps to your right.

The Other Man: Sorry?

The Man: Back. Not like that. Go backwards. Ok. Now jump.

The Other Man: What? Ah come on now.

The Man: Jump.

The Other Man: Where?

The Man: Backwards and forwards. Several times.

The Other Man: (*Jumps*) Is that enough?

The Man: Once more.

The Other Man: (*Disoriented*) I'm tired.

The Man: All right.

The Other Man: How did I do?

The Man: Look …I've got a mission for you.

The Other Man: (*Flattered*) For me?

The Man: It must stay between us.

The Other Man: I'm dumb … so to speak.

The Man: But first of all I need to tell you something. (*Beat*) I am immortal.

Pause. The Other Man is in awe.

The Man: I haven't grown since I was twelve. Unchanged. I didn't notice until recently. But I've been studying myself very carefully.

The Other Man: You seem older.

The Man: You mean physically? Of course, but that doesn't matter to me. It's what's inside that counts. What's important is how I feel, not how I look.

The Other Man: (*Innocently*) That's just as well. Because you don't look that great.

The Man gives him a dirty look.

The Other Man: I'm sorry, what I meant was –

The Man: The first rule of our partnership is that you listen to me until I'm finished. No matter what I tell you or how long it takes. Is that clear?

The Other Man: (*Nods*) Just a suggestion, but shouldn't we go and hide somewhere? What if it starts raining just when it's getting important? I'm always getting caught in the rain when things are really important.

The Man: So what if it rains? People fought and died on the front line and you didn't hear them complaining.

The Other Man: I wanted to go too but there was no war on. What could I do?

The Man: Start one.

The Other Man: With what? I didn't even have a gun.

The Man: With your mind.

The Other Man: I prefer atomic wars to psychological ones. They don't hurt my head as much.

The Man: Then keep quiet. As an alien I am your superior. If you challenge me, you'll be sorry.

The Other Man: Oh my God.

The Man: You're safe for the moment. (*Beat*) I need your help.

The Other Man: Anything at all. I love being helpful.

The Man: Do you think our meeting was a matter of chance?

The Other Man: Wasn't it?

The Man: No. I realized that while talking to you.

The Other Man: Really?

The Man: I need someone I can trust.

The Other Man: Stop looking, you found him! At your service!

The Man: Without realizing it, you've passed some tests.

The Other Man: Have I?

The Man: Quiet! I'm doing the talking. I've studied you very carefully. With every word you've chased away every doubt that I had about you. You have come into my life at exactly the right time.

The Other Man: You're scaring me! I'm a bit faint-hearted at the best of times.

The Man: Shut up! All the signals are there. The atmosphere has been getting more and more tense. The silence becoming heavier and heavier. And a strange echo has been almost making my ears bleed.

The Other Man: Is that my fault? I didn't do anything, I swear.

The Man: One more interruption and everything turns to dust! Be warned! We are experiencing a moment of … astronomical significance. There's no turning back. We can't hide from the truth. Your next step could change the face of the Earth … Are you ready to discover the greatest mystery of your life? The real thing that keeps you awake at night?

The Other Man: May I answer?

The Man: Yes, please.

The Other Man: I am ready.

The Man: Don't be hasty. What you're about to find out will change your entire existence.

The Other Man: When I said yes, I meant yes.

The Man: You should think it over ten times before you give me an answer. Trust me.

The Other Man: We have no time for that. Once is enough. I'm not messing with you. I'm a man of my word.

The Man: You are Spiderman.

Pause.

The Other Man: Come again?!

The Man: You are Spiderman. You know – the guy who climbs up buildings. The one I've been waiting for. My fellow extraterrestrial. My purpose in life.

The Other Man: Who? Me?

The Man: It's obvious. There's no point denying it. Give up this pathetic delusion. Your place is not among humans. You have to assume your real identity. Lucky you, you are born again. Fulfil your destiny.

The Other Man: I suffer from vertigo.

The Man: You did. Because you didn't know. Now things have become clear. You can even fly.

The Other Man: Am I allowed?

The Man: You don't need permission. Get up and fly!

The Other Man: Like Black Beauty? But I don't eat fire.

The Man: That's irrelevant! Knowing that you can fly is enough.

The Other Man is on his feet and is about to flap his wings.

The Man: But you must keep it secret. (*The Other Man sits*) If you fly around all day, people will get used to it and it'll become boring. Or they'll try to stop you and pull you down.

The Other Man: They wouldn't dare …

The Man: It's no joke. People can be really hurtful when they want to be. Really mean. (*Becoming instrospective*) This country is full of begrudgers, always dragging you down when you're trying to do something special. Stupid, ignorant bastards.

The Man, upset, turns away and takes out his razorblade sharpening tool and begins to sharpen a razorblade. The Other Man watches sympathetically for some moments, then reaches out and touches The Man on the arm in a bid to calm him that slowly works.

The Other Man: But I'm not scared of them. Especially now.

The Man: Yes, you're not the same as before. You're much more powerful now. You have supernatural abilities.

The Other Man: I can feel them.

The Man: Don't waste them. Use them only when they're needed.

The Other Man: Can I move furniture? I could earn us some money.

The Man: What good would money do? Money won't solve anything.

The Other Man: I'm sorry, I didn't mean to offend you. But how can I use my powers? I'm afraid I don't understand.

The Man: You'll know when the time comes.

A third man, ***The Human Wreck,*** *appears, very distraught, unhinged and quite dangerous. He is holding an accordion. He is younger than The Other Man.*

The Man: Quiet. Were you waiting for someone?

The Other Man: No.

The Man: Maybe he's been here for a while. Do you think he heard us?

The Other Man: I don't think so. I think I would have noticed. My hearing is better now, isn't it?

The Man: No, not yet. I'll let you know when.

The Wreck: I'm such a wreck. My wife has run away with my Father. My Mother with my wife's brother. My sister with the sports teacher. My brother with his stepdaughter. And I'm in love with my grandfather's wife. His fourth wife. Meanwhile, my grandfather married my Father's second wife. My younger brother's first wife. Who is now married to our first cousin. The sports teacher's ex-lover, since he was married to my present wife. The bitch who ran away with my Father. (*Starts crying*)

The Man: Is he talking to us?

The Other Man: I think he's talking to himself. It happens to me sometimes.

The Wreck: If my grandfather hadn't broken up with his fourth wife and my Mother hadn't fallen in love with my wife's brother, I would be living happily near my wife and with our first cousin, first wife of the sports teacher and present wife of my little brother, who's madly in love with his boss anyway.

The Man: Did you get any of that?

The Other Man: Did you?

The Man: Something about his family …

The Other Man: His family is a mess.

The Wreck: (*To them*) I've been deeply in love with her since the second grade. In the days when she was in love with the Schoolmaster, the husband of the librarian who has a child with my older brother.

The Other Man: Who's he talking about? His wife?

The Man: No. His first cousin who is married to his brother.

The Other Man: Who?

The Man: The one who was married to the sports teacher.

The Wreck: I spent three years caring for the sports teacher's baby, thinking it was mine. How wrong I was. His ears and his hands are exactly like his Father's. I can't believe that my wife left me. And for who? My Father?!

The Other Man: He's talking about his wife.

The Wreck: If only I could have married a woman like my Mother. What a woman my Mother was when she was young. Everybody tells me that – 'What a woman'. When we went out in the street together everybody came to say hello. Well except for the other women, but they were just jealous. All the men – from bell-boy to president.

The Other Man: The President?

The Wreck: President of the local football club, but still. And she was so polite to everybody. She would smile at everybody. Most of them were just left speechless and would wink and nudge each other when they saw her. They were obviously in awe of her wonderful smile. But she never smiled at my Father. Nobody did, really. He wasn't a great smiler himself either. Later in his life he managed to improve. Now the whole city is full of his smile. Everybody smiles like him. Everybody but me. My smile is more like that of a famous actor, who used to visit my Mother when my Father was away. We have all his movies on tape, at home. My Mother loved those movies, my Father didn't. I wonder why?

The Other Man: Maybe he preferred other actors.

The Man: Shut up!

The Wreck: Who knows?! I feel so tired.

The Man: I noticed. Why don't you sit here for a while?

The Wreck: I can't sit.

The Man: You can't or you won't?

The Wreck: Why do you want to know that?

The Man: No particular reason, I'm just curious.

The Wreck: I can't. I have something stuck up my arse.

The Other Man: Are you serious? (*To The Man*) I knew there was something wrong with him. Maybe your friends paid him a visit?

The Man: How dare you! As if they haven't got better things to be doing. And remember, they're your friends too now. (*To The Wreck*) What exactly happened to you?

The Other Man: Did you do something wrong?

The Wreck: (*Affronted*) What do you mean?

The Other Man: Do you have a big mouth? Did you let slip a big secret? Who are you in fact, if you don't mind us asking?

The Wreck: Florian Pittis.

The Other Man: Who?

The Man: The famous actor.

The Other Man: Never heard of him.

The Man: Or is he a famous footballer?

The Other Man: So what is he – a famous actor or a famous footballer?

The Man: What are you – the famous actor or the famous footballer?

The Wreck: You know what? It gives me absolutely no pleasure to meet you. So don't tell me your names because I'll forget them anyway. (*Pause*) But you did recognize me, didn't you?

The Other Man: Well –

The Wreck: All this suffering has changed me. I wish I'd never met you. I'm leaving, anyway.

The Man: Stay with us for a while. You've only just got here and already you want to leave?

The Wreck: I want to die.

The Other Man: Oh …

The Man: Aren't you a little bit young? You've got your whole life ahead of you.

The Wreck: It's my only hope. Life has brought me nothing but misery. It's been torture, ever since I was born. I always wanted the things that I couldn't have and I was only offered the things I didn't want. I'm telling you, everything is in vain. No matter what you try to do, you always realize that you wanted something else. And it always happens exactly when you think you're the happiest man alive. You'll end up like me.

The Man: It'll pass.

The Wreck: And then what? Other problems will appear.

The Man: They'll pass as well.

The Wreck: But I'm so tired. I don't believe in fairytales anymore. I was serious when I told you I was Florian Pittis. Only I'm not the famous one. I'm just another guy with the same name. Isn't that pathetic? I feel like shit. Thank God my name isn't Adolf Hitler. Then again, if my name was Adolf Hitler I'd probably want it to be Florian Pittis … And if my name was Florian Pittis, I'd want it to be Adolf Hitler.

The Man: But your name is Florian Pittis?

The Other Man: (*To The Man*) This guy is one of those masochists, that's for sure.

The Wreck: (*Pulls a piece of rope out of his pocket*) Anyway, I'm going to kill myself. Not here, in front of you. I refuse to give you a reason to celebrate. Or to pity me. I refuse to give you anything, to be honest. I'll find a quieter place. And sadder. Not even a rat could commit suicide here. Or a chicken. I realized that the moment I laid eyes on you. I have to tell you something. You are the ugliest people I have ever met. (*To The Man*) Especially you. I don't regret at all not getting to know you two.

The Man and The Other Man look at each other. The Wreck is about to leave.

The Wreck: I've never done anything important in my life, so I don't expect the world to cry for me. I never intended to either. And I don't regret it a bit.

He starts to leave, then turns around and drops the accordion at their feet.

The Wreck: I'll leave you my accordion, there's no point taking it with me. The bases are damaged. You can play it if you want. It could be useful for my hanging, it's quite heavy, but I think I can manage without it. I shall die thinking of the woman I love, not holding her in my arms.

The Other Man: (*Innocently*) Or thinking that someone else is holding her in their arms?

The Wreck: I think it's better this way. Holding her as I died wouldn't be any great shakes either.

The Other Man: The weight of her would break your arms.

The Wreck: Tell all my friends that I thank them. For helping me when I didn't need help and for not helping me when I did. Goodbye.

He slaps both of them across the ears and then leaves. The slap has a particularly strong effect on The Man, appearing to stir some kind of realization in him.

The Other Man: If I didn't know he was going to kill himself, I think I'd have done it.

The Man: Shut up. Don't you get it?

The Other Man: Maybe he didn't hit you as hard, but my ears are still ringing.

The Man: Your ears are ringing?

The Other Man: Badly.

The Man: Why do you think they're ringing?

The Other Man: Because he hit me.

The Man: I don't think that's the reason. I think he was the sign.

The Other Man: What sign?

The Man: The one that I've been waiting for.

The Other Man: Are you serious? But what were the slaps for?

The Man: Do you think I'm in the mood for joking?

The Other Man: Of course not, but –

The Man: Let's go after him.

The Other Man: Wait! It might be a trap.

The Human Wreck re-enters.

The Man: (*To The Other Man*) Leave it to me.

The Wreck: I've changed my mind. I can't leave you the accordion. Do you mind?

The Other Man: No problem. It's broken anyway.

The Man: (*To The Other Man*) Shh.

The Wreck: Typical. You just want rid of me as soon as possible – you want to forget you ever met me.

The Other Man: We thought you had something to do.

The Wreck: And you couldn't care less, could you? How can you be so indifferent? Do you think I'm the only one who suffers from love?

The Other Man: Maybe there are other people too. They probably don't go on about it as much, though.

The Man: (*Placating The Wreck*) I'm sure there are. Statistically speaking.

The Man is silent during the following onslaught.

The Wreck: You two have never been in love. There's no doubt about it. What is the meaning of your lives? Have you ever thought about that? What is your purpose? Why were you born? There is a reason, isn't there?

The Other Man: Of course.

The Wreck: So you have goals? Why didn't you say so? I bow before your necessity on this planet. I bet you just stare at the stars all night and sleep during the day. I bet you're just shadows on the Earth during the winter, and no good to anyone. And then what? You rest all summer? You useless clowns! Do you have any children?

The Other Man: Not yet.

The Wreck: What a stupid question! Of course not. How can you have children on your own? Why am I wasting my time even talking to you? (*Pause*) I couldn't find any trees around here. That's why I came back. Under these circumstances, I can't hang myself.

The Other Man: There are other ways.

The Wreck: I don't care about other ways. Death by hanging is the most romantic.

The Other Man: If you say so.

The Wreck: You've got to help me.

The Other Man: We were just about to leave.

The Wreck: No you're not, because I have a gun. (*Takes out the gun*) And if you don't help me I'm going to shoot you.

The Other Man: Why didn't you tell us that in the first place? That changes everything. We'll find a solution. We can be very inventive when we want to be, can't we?

The Man is silent.

The Wreck: I thought so. Here's what we're going to do. I'll tie the rope around my neck and then each of you will pull an end until you see my tongue coming out.

The Other Man: That's going to be very romantic.

The Wreck: Isn't it? Let's give it a try first. (*To The Other Man*) Tie the rope around your neck. Quickly.

The Other Man: But I have a very short neck. What am I saying, I hardly have a neck. I mean I don't think I have a neck at all. You call this a neck?

The Man: What about my neck?

The Wreck: I don't care who's neck it is.

The Man takes the rope and puts it around his own neck. The Other Man is horrified.

The Man: Is this tight enough?

The Wreck: Perfect! (*To The Other Man*) Now pick up the other end.

The Other Man doesn't know what to do.

The Wreck: Do it!

The Man nods to The Other Man, who picks up the rope.

The Wreck: Now pull!

The Wreck and The Other Man pull the rope, which tightens around the neck of The Man, who stands between them. The Other Man, greatly distressed, pulls with only half a heart, The Wreck with considerable strength.

The Wreck: Harder!

They pull harder. The Man buckles and falls to his knees.

The Wreck: Stop! Ok. Let's see your tongue! Well done! And the eyes! Both of them! That's it, that's it. Looks good. I approve. Now let's pull the rope another bit. You're clearly in pain. Roll your eyes. And the tongue. Good.

The Wreck approaches, holding the gun to the head of The Man, standing over him.

The Wreck: Now I'll have a go. How was it?

The Man doesn't answer. The Other Man goes to his aid.

The Wreck: Not very pleasant, I'd say. You see I have to suffer. It has to be dramatic. Tragic. Horrifying.

The Men remain silent.

The Wreck: Terrifying.

The Other Man helps The Man onto the bench.

The Wreck: Monstrous. And at the same time monumental. (*Pause, distressed that he's being ignored*) Suffocating even. (*Pause*) Can I ask you something?

The Other Man: What now?

The Wreck: I want you to witness my death. I don't want to die all alone.

The Other Man: With pleasure. (*Pause*) Believe me, I know what loneliness is.

The Wreck: Really? What is it?

The Other Man: Being alone is dreadful. Not having someone to bring you a glass of water when you're thirsty. Not having someone to talk to. Not having someone to help you. Like now.

The Wreck: Go on …

The Other Man: Eating alone. Sleeping alone. Waking alone and then eating again. Sleeping again and waking again. And then once more … and always, day after day. No one to contradict you. No one to quarrel with you. No one to ask you anything. Whatever you do, no one to be interested. No one to bring a glass of water to. To discover the healing sexual act and to have no-one to share it with.

The Wreck: Your turn now.

The Man: I just wanted to help.

The Wreck: Loneliness. Tell me about loneliness.

The Man: Well …

The Wreck: Yes?

The Man: Loneliness is a complex …what's the word … and sinuous group of misunderstandings that makes you …

The Other Man: Spend your time alone. Am I wrong?

The Wreck: Shut up! (*To The Man*) You go on …

The Man: Where was I? I lost it.

The Wreck: Already? Search for it.

The Man: Loneliness is …

The Other Man: Tough. What am I saying, it's very tough. Incredibly tough. Not easy at all. On the contrary.

The Wreck: I know it's tough, but …

The Other Man: And big. As a mountain.

The Wreck: (*To The Man*) And?

The Other Man: Should I only refer to people?

The Wreck: I'm not interested in plants.

The Other Man: I wasn't talking about plants.

The Wreck: Shut up! (*To The Man*) Go on, please.

The Man: That's all.

Pause.

The Wreck: That's all?

The Man shrugs. The Other Man does the same.

The Wreck: There will be plenty of loneliness after I shoot you both. How about that? Am I right about that?

The Other Man: Yes. You're right. There would be.

The Man: Well it depends.

The Wreck: I think I'll shoot you first.

The Man: (*Calmly*) Why?

The Wreck: Why not? Because I don't like the look of you, that's why. Have you got a problem with that? You look like a lunatic. What are you two doing here at this hour anyway? Enlighten me.

The Other Man: I thought you had other plans.

The Wreck: I changed my mind. I'd rather kill you two. Much more entertaining for me. Maybe it would make me forget about my loneliness.

The Other Man: But you'd be all alone.

The Wreck: And what am I right now?

The Other Man: You're with us.

The Man: You are not alone anymore.

Pause.

The Wreck: Are you members of a sect or something? Do you drink your own piss and stuff like that?

The Man: Maybe.

The Wreck: Yes or no?

The Other Man: Yes we are.

The Man: No. We don't know.

The Other Man: We don't remember.

The Wreck: Yes or no?

The Man: Who can say?

The Wreck: You're so annoying. If you had any idea how hard it is for me not to shoot you. I think it would really help me.

The Other Man: I don't think he'd be that easy to kill.

The Wreck: How about you?

The Other Man: I don't know. I've never tried.

The Wreck gives up in frustration and turns away.

The Wreck: It's so difficult for me. I miss her so much. I'm just wrecked. Whenever I think of her, I lose my courage. She's stolen my heart. She's inside my head. Messing up my thoughts. Like a thief. Leave me alone! What can I do?

The Man: Well hanging yourself would be a solution of sorts.

The Wreck: But if I die I'll never see her again.

The Man: You'd be rid of her for good, but...

The Wreck: That's what I want. No! I'd still want to see her, even in the afterlife.

The Other Man: Then why not shoot her too? That way you could still meet.

The Wreck: Never! Can't you understand that I love her?

The Man: Wouldn't it be better if you shot them?

The Wreck: Them? Who?

The Man: The people who hurt you. Your family. It sounds like they're the cause of all your problems.

The Other Man: Yeah … What a mess … One big happy family, isn't it? A bit crowded, it sounds like.

The Wreck: You're telling me to shoot my own family?

The Man: Not everybody. Only the guilty ones.

The Wreck: I don't get it.

The Man: It's simple. Who did your wife run away with?

The Wreck: My Father.

The Man: So …

The Wreck: I should shoot my Father?

The Man: You see. Piece of cake.

The Other Man: It would save you a lot of trouble.

The Man: Of course it's just an idea …

The Wreck: It would cause a huge scandal. Do you have any idea who my father is?

The Other Man: I haven't had the pleasure.

The Wreck: I couldn't.

The Man: Why?

The Wreck: I love him. He's my own flesh and blood. The man who gave me life. My Father.

The Man: Okay, so killing your Father is out of the question?

The Wreck: Absolutely. (*Pause*) I'm sorry.

The Man: No, it's okay. It just makes things a bit complicated.

The Wreck: What do you mean?

The Man: You have to kill her instead.

The Other Man: The wife? No way.

The Man: I'm sorry to say it, but she's the most guilty.

The Other Man: I think the Father should die. To kidnap your wife, acting like a teenager … No way, that just isn't right. What are we? Indians, outlaws, savages?

The Man: She ran away with him, not him with her. Am I right?

The Wreck: I don't know who did what. Does it matter?

The Man: Can't you see the difference? Her planning it is one thing – him planning it is quite another.

The Other Man: Absolutely. Who was behind it?

The Wreck is confused.

The Man: Well?

The Wreck: I have no idea.

The Man: Make up your mind. Otherwise you're wasting our time.

The Wreck: It's all my fault. I'm in love with my grandfather's wife. Not my wife. My wife is free to run away with whoever she wants, I don't care.

The Man: What? You mean we've just wrecked our heads for nothing? (*Beat*) Then you'll have to shoot the grandfather.

The Wreck: No. My grandfather doesn't love his wife anymore. He's in love with my Father's second wife.

The Other Man: See, I was right. The Father has to be shot.

The Man: No, the grandfather.

The Other Man: But why?

The Man: Because he gave life to his son!

The Other Man: What son?

The Man: His Father. Who ran away with the wife.

The Other Man: So?

The Man: It's all his fault. He should have been a better father.

The Other Man: The grandfather is old. Fathers are always responsible, never grandfathers. He's got to go.

The Wreck: I don't understand a thing.

The Man: Let's sit for a minute. For me it is crystal clear. Let's go through all of it once again. You're in love with your grandfather's wife, and your grandfather loves the second wife of your Father, who ran away with your wife.

The Other Man: Who did the wife run away with?

The Man: Whose wife?

The Other Man: His wife.

The Wreck: With my Father. But I wasn't in love with her anymore. I helped her to run away.

The Man: You did? Then where's the problem?

The Wreck: I don't know anymore.

The Other Man: I know. You love your grandfather's wife.

The Wreck: No. I'm just having an affair with her. I'm in love with my brother's wife.

The Man: Who's that?

The Wreck: Florence. Our cousin.

The Man: Florence? That changes everything.

The Other Man: Wait! Did you just say cousin?

The Wreck: Yes. First cousin. My Mother's brother's daughter.

The Other Man: But that's wrong. That's not allowed.

The Wreck: I know. That's exactly the problem.

The Other Man: Who do you think you are, Alexander the Great?

The Man: He means Caligula.

The Wreck: I'm sorry. But I'm in love with her.

The Other Man: I'm sorry too, but that's just not on.

The Wreck: Then what can I do?

The Man: Go home and take a nap. We can't do anything right now. It's too late.

The Wreck: That's why I want to shoot myself.

The Man: There's no need anymore.

The Wreck: How come?

The Man: The relationship is impossible. Incestuous almost. There's no point suffering. Does she know?

The Other Man: Wait a minute. Who?

The Man: Cousin Florence.

The Wreck: No. And I wouldn't want her to. It's not right.

The Other Man: Go home and sleep. Please.

The Wreck: But I'm not sleepy. I'd like to stay another bit. Please …

The Man and The Other Man consider this and decide.

The Man: Ok, but not for long.

The Wreck: Whatever you say.

The Wreck sits on the bench. The Man, satisfied, removes his shoes and stretches his feet, wriggling his toes. The Other Man does the same. The Wreck looks at their feet and at The Other Man, who nods that it's okay for the Wreck to copy them. The Wreck removes his shoes, revealing expensive socks, which The Other Man admires enviously.

The Man: (*Like a guru*) Love-love, I can see that, but you can go too far … Sometimes you change your mind. Or you just realize you've made the wrong choice. Once is forgivable. Ok, twice. Three times … maybe. But in your case, it's quite serious. And you're all like that. Family heritage … What a mess …

The Wreck: It's like a virus. If it gets into your blood, you're lost.

The Other Man: Are your brothers the same as you?

The Wreck: Yes.

The Man: You're all infected.

The Other Man: I hope it's not contagious, God help us! What if I fall in love with my Mother? Poor old woman …

The Man: Stay calm. There's no need to worry. (*Pause*) I think morning is upon us.

The Other Man: But you can still see the moon.

The Man: Haven't you learnt anything?

The Other Man: Oh. Yes, of course.

The Man: I suggest we get some sleep.

The Man puts his shoes back on. The Other Man does the same.

The Wreck: I can't sleep, don't you understand?

The Man: Here's what we'll do. Tomorrow, at the same time, you bring all of them here.

The Other Man: Yes, bring Florence.

The Man: We'll clarify things and solve the problem. We'll be rested by then.

The Wreck: Tomorrow? What about the accordion?

The Man: I don't think you'll need it anymore.

The Other Man: Listen to him. Bring all your family here tomorrow night. There's no other way.

The Man: Ok?

The Wreck nods reluctantly.

The Man: Goodbye now. Goodnight. Here's your rope. You can throw it away. After all, you don't need it.

The Other Man: Might be better to hide it here somewhere. You never know …

The Man grabs the rope and throws it away. Pause. The Other Man becomes anxious.

The Other Man: (*Trying to sound casual*) So, what now?

The Man: (*Reassuring him*) Just wait one moment.

The Other Man moves off, but not too far.

The Man: (*To The Wreck*) We're leaving now. (*The Wreck looks lonely*) Come on, cheer up, be a man. Don't let us down. Go home and get some sleep. (*Moves closer, speaks in confidence*) I don't want to go into it now, but I'll tell you something important about yourself tomorrow … something that will change your entire existence. You'll be able to see all your problems as insignificant little details.

The Wreck nods gravely.

The Man: Could you stand up, please? Now sit. Get up again. Wave your hands a bit. Harder. Aha. I see. Now blink a few times. Quicker. Very good. Let me see your tongue. Now, look at me and do this. Turn around. Your face too. Yes, it's clear. We'll talk again tomorrow, after we've solved that mess. Stand up again. Now go. Goodnight.

The Wreck exits. The Man sits on the bench. The Other Man looks at him uncertainly. The Man nods and The Other Man joins him on the bench, delighted.

The Voice: Betty! You're here! (*Crying*) Where were you? … I missed you so much … Come to daddy! I won't hurt you. You left me here all alone, like a fool. You pretended not to hear me. Come on, bring me the ball! Come on, let's play! Bring me the ball! I know you understand me. Where are you going? Betty! Bring me the ball, do you hear me?! You stupid animal! Don't you do that in here. Don't you crap in here! Get out! Get out or I'll kick you up the arse! Stop it, you flea-bag! Get out! Out!

Blackout.

The End

Our Father Who Art in the Supermarket

By Petre Barbu

Translated by Andrei Marinescu
Adapted by Paul Meade

Characters:

Radu Onica, 54
Bogdan Onica, 25, Radu's son from a previous marriage
Sorin Petric, around 40
Roxana, 35, Radu's second wife
The Mad Dogs – a gang from the neighbourhood
Old pensioners and other poor people

ACT I

SCENE 1: Bogdan's studio apartment

Radu: This place smells like a toilet.

Bogdan: Your sausages are off.

Radu: No, they're fresh, I only got them this morning from Nicu the butcher.

Bogdan: He screwed you.

Radu: Well isn't it lucky there's a sausage expert in the family? (*Goes to the bathroom*) Oh, Jesus! What's going on in here?! (*We hear him flushing the toilet*) You didn't flush!

Bogdan: I forgot.

Radu: Forgot my arse! Bogdan, this is … you're living like an animal!

Bogdan: I've had diarrhoea for two days. Are you eating those sausages or will I throw them away?

Radu: What do you mean throw them away? Put them in the fridge. I can't eat them now, I've lost my appetite.

Bogdan: It's broken, the motor's banjaxed.

Radu: Where are you gonna keep my sausages then?

Bogdan: In the loo, it's cooler in there.

Radu: Why didn't you tell me about the fridge, I could have brought my tools and fixed the belt.

Bogdan: Dad! Your getting on my tits now!

Radu: Ok, Bogdan! If I'm boring you, I'll just go to my whores.

Bogdan: And I'll tell Roxana and get you in the shit!

Radu: Oh, God, look what it's come to, turned in by my own son! Go on tell her if you want to, she'll add it to my file, you little securitate snitch!

Bogdan: Listen, I'll take you to any movie you want if you just stop wrecking my head!

Radu: You know, Bogdan, it's strange, sometimes I really miss a good old communist movie. One with prime-secretaries, lathe operators and model workers, laughing my arse off seeing comrade Ion, the welder and comrade Elena, the factory girl, walking hand in hand in the park. And then we'd all shout, 'Fuck her, fuck her!'.

Bogdan: Is that what you were up to when you took Mum to the movies?

Radu: Your Mother was an intellectual. And anyway if you shouted that in the communist days, the police would have busted you like that! Ah, you haven't a clue …! You know, now would be the perfect time to rent a cinema in town and show some good flicks from the National Archives. We could even open a small shop in the foyer, with sweets and minerals. What do you think, let's make some money, are you with me? Are you in?

Bogdan: Dad, you've got Roxana and her son to support. You look after your health and your job. Retirement is just around the corner.

Radu: I get it, I'm too old to make money, am I? Only your man, Mitica, is allowed go into business? That mangey policeman, that prick has bought you off, hasn't he?

Bogdan: Mitica was never in the police.

Radu: No not the police. People say he was a captain in the *old police*. The Militia. And now he's a businessman, buying everyone off, including you.

Bogdan: I told you, I'm delivering some packages for him, that's all. He's paying me fair and square.

Radu: Wouldn't you come to my cinema to see 'Hello from Agigea'? It's all about a boy who runs off to the Canal to work as a digger and becomes a worthy son of the Socialist Republic of Romania. Now his girl is studying Medicine and waits lovingly for him while doing the bold thing with a classmate? Ha ha ha, that was fab!

Bogdan: No.

Radu: But why? Ok, you're a student, I'll give you a student discount.

Bogdan: Because I'm not interested.

Radu: You're stupid. You just don't know how to enjoy yourself. You'll be Mitica's ballboy all your life. You'll die in this place with its broken fridge and smelly loo. Even your accountancy diploma won't give you a pot to piss in.

Bogdan: I could become a 'brand manager'.

Radu: What's that?

Bogdan: It's a kind of very well paid salesman who kisses ass to sell his stuff.

Radu: Your Mother would have killed me if she heard you talking like this.

Bogdan: Let me tell you something, and I'm glad Mum's not alive to hear this: you have to make a delivery for Mitica tonight.

Radu: You want me to be the policeman's errand boy now?

Bogdan: He's not a policeman.

Radu: Old police. I'm telling you, he was old police.

Bogdan: Look, Sorin Petric will go with you.

Radu: Who's that?

Bogdan: He's just a guy who helps with the deliveries. You find the address, ring the bell, Sorin delivers the package and then you leave. And this is important, don't look at the guy who takes the stuff.

Radu: Should I close my eyes?

Bogdan: Just don't look at him. Three or four deliveries. In three hours you'll be free.

Radu: Why can't you do it?

Bogdan: I've got diarrhoea and I don't feel well. You'll get fifty dollars. Why should I give fifty dollars to some stranger, when my Father could have it?

Radu: Are you giving fifty dollars to your Father?

Bogdan: Sure, you could pay your maintenance, the electricity bill.

Radu: What would I tell Roxana?

Bogdan: That you fixed my fridge, you had something to drink and you fell asleep here, in my place …

Five masked soldiers break into the apartment.

Soldier 1: Put your hands up! Everybody, face the wall and hands up!

Radu: But why, wha …

Soldier 2: Shut up! Face the wall, hands up! Don't move!

Soldier 3: Bathroom clear!

Soldier 4: Kitchen clear!

Radu: What did I do? …

Soldier 5: Shut up! Turn around!

Soldiers 2 and 5 are searching Radu and Bogdan. They throw everything on the floor – identity cards, wallets, keys etc. Soldier 2 finds a penknife in Radu's pocket.

Soldier 2: Gun!

Radu: That's a penknife, I use it to cut bread and sausages for my lunch. Bogdan, tell them, I just used it to cut those sausages from Nicu the butcher!

Soldier 1: Shut up! I have to confiscate it as evidence for the trial.

Radu: What trial?

Soldier 1: In the name of the law, Radu Onica, I am placing you under arrest!

Radu: For what?

Soldier 1: Terrorist activities. Planting bombs in the town square. (*To Soldier 2*) Search him!

Radu: What bombs? I'm a qualified worker at the Optical Institute. Why would I plant bombs in the town square?

Soldier 1: (*Slaps him across the face*) Shut up! Take your clothes off and turn your arsehole to the light!

Radu takes his clothes off.

SCENE 2: Radu's apartment

Bogdan: I thought I was going to get sick when I saw his dry little sack.

Roxana: Don't be cruel!

Bogdan: I just wanted to see what I came out of, before entering my Mother's womb.

Roxana: And you paid thirty dollars to find that out?

Bogdan: The Mad Dogs are really bad actors: 'Hands up! Everybody hands up!' What a bunch of queers! I only gave them 20 dollars, for vodka.

Roxana: He could have had a heart attack.

Bogdan: He was proud as a peacock when I pretended I was calling Mitica on the phone to fix it with the police. You should have seen his face when the Mad Dogs apologized, saying it was just a terrible misunderstanding. 'Please excuse us, Mister Onica!'

Roxana: You humiliated him.

Bogdan: I gave him a moment of excitement.

Roxana: And when you get him excited, he comes home and crashes out like a drunk. I have to drag him out of bed in the morning to get him to work. And in the afternoon, he sits there like a vegetable, watching TV, complaining about all his aches and pains.

Bogdan: Did he go on about beating me at tennis?

Roxana: You let him win.

Bogdan: No, honestly, he really beat me. He was hitting the ball as if it was my head. Then he lets a roar out of him like a lion when he wins match point! We went to the pub afterwards and he got drunk. Didn't he tell you? He got pissed on two beers and he starts singing karaoke. On the table! Al Bano and Tom Jones. I'm not joking he was loving it.

Roxana: And you?

Bogdan: I don't really give a bollox.

Roxana: Liar! You made him take his clothes off to make sure he can't get it up.

Bogdan: I'm better than him, aren't I?

Roxana: You've no technique.

Bogdan: Does he?

Roxana: I'm not going there.

Bogdan: What about a threesome?

Roxana: Why not with your Mother?

Bogdan: My Mother satisfied him, because she was an intellectual.

Roxana: If your Mother was still alive, you'd probably take her clothes off, to see which hole you came out!

Bogdan: Tell me again how that truck driver got you up the duff with Ionut.

Roxana: I don't remember.

Bogdan: Come on, you don't remember how drunk he was when he shagged you?

Roxana: The next day, he beat me and he took off in his truck. A week later he came back, but I'd already moved to my Mother's.

Bogdan: And then you replaced him with my Father, because he's got technique.

Roxana: Are you holding me responsible for something, little boy?

Bogdan: I never understood why my Mother and Father got married.

Roxana: Love.

Bogdan: Bullshit. My Mother wasn't the type to marry a fool like him.

Roxana: You don't know what she felt when she met Radu.

Bogdan: Oh, yeah? What did you feel?

Roxana: I liked him.

Bogdan: Come on, don't give me that bullshit! You just couldn't raise Ionut on a sales-girl's salary in a second-hand clothes shop!

Roxana: What about your teacher Mother or whatever she was, with her fancy foreign languages. Why did she marry him?

Bogdan: That's what kills me, 'cause I don't know. I'm pissed off 'cause I've only seen my Mother in photographs. Is that what I'm related to, those bloody photographs? Why were they attracted to each other? What was in it for them, because there must have been something if they had me.

Roxana: Radu was proud to have an intellectual wife.

Bogdan: Forget it, you don't even know what intellectual means ...

Someone flushes the toilet next door. Roxana leaves the room. Bogdan listens. He searches his pockets and takes out a few notes. Roxana comes back.

Roxana: Ionut's in the bathroom, his tummy's sore. I don't know what to do with him anymore, I've taken him to so many doctors ... Where are you going?

Bogdan: Here's some money for Ionut.

Roxana: There's no need. I already bought his pills.

Bogdan: For school stuff, then, you'll need it ... Don't look at me like that. It's from his stepbrother, it's no big deal.

Roxana: (*Takes the money*) Don't take Radu to the pub anymore.

Bogdan: Why don't you try keeping him home more, I am running out of ways to entertain him.

Roxana: What about us?

Bogdan: I'm gonna have my own supermarket and I'll make you head of the cosmetics department. You'll see, it's gonna be grand.

Roxana: Swear you'll never get bored of me!

Bogdan: Ok, I'll swear on anything you want.

Roxana: On your Mother.

SCENE 3: A street in the suburbs.

Sorin: Excuse me, Radu, could you check at that end, where the green light is please?

Radu: I've already been there, there's no 253.

Sorin: Maybe you missed it.

Radu: Are you deaf my friend? There's no 253! You're not only deaf you're blind: that light's not green, it's blue.

Sorin: Ok, Grandad, go to the other end then …

Radu: Listen here, if you call me 'Grandad' again you'll be picking your teeth out of my boot! Call the guy who gave you the address and tell him he's thick. There's no 253 on this Street.

Sorin: I don't have his number.

Radu: Okay, okay. Then I'll go knock on one of these doors and ask them where's 253.

Sorin: Don't do that! People can't know where we're looking for.

Radu: What kind of gangsters are you guys? You can't even deliver the drugs!

Sorin: They're not drugs, it's merchandise.

Radu: Yeah, right, you believe that. You and all the idiots that work for Mitica! Was it you dragged Bogdan into this trafficking filth?

Sorin: We've only known each other for two weeks, when we started making these deliveries together.

Radu: Where did you work before that?

Sorin: Nowhere.

Radu: Are you a handicap or something?

Sorin: Well I had all the childhood diseases.

Radu: Ok, now I get it, you're a parasite. Ceausescu used to arrest all the parasites and take them to dig the canal. How did you manage to avoid working?

Sorin: Nothing really appealed to me. I just couldn't find my place, I didn't fit in, I wasn't able to choose, I didn't look, I had no luck …

Radu: Don't you have a wife, children?

Sorin: I'm alone.

Radu: Bogdan's alone too … Are you sure you're not some sort of a pansy, teaching him filthy tricks …

Sorin: We have to find number 253!

Radu: Let's just throw the package down the drain and you tell them that we took it to the right place, it's not like we signed for it or anything …

Sorin: They keep a record.

Radu: I'm going to the police, then!

Sorin: Mitica's people won't forget you did this.

Radu: Mister Sorin Petric, we've only just met. I was just taking a stroll, because of my insomnia and I ended up on this street. You asked me where number 253 was and I shrugged. I didn't even see your face. Then you went towards that green light, can you see it, and I went back home and I went to sleep beside my wife. Good night!

Sorin: Bogdan might be in for it if we don't find 253.

Radu: Why don't we come back in the morning and find the bloody address in daylight!

Sorin: We have to find it right now. That's the rule.

Radu: Sorin my son, if it's so important, then let's have a look inside the package, and see what's there!

Sorin: It's sealed, look.

Radu: This is what I get for selling my soul for fifty dollars! …

Sorin: Who's giving you fifty dollars?

Radu: What do you mean who? Mitica!

Sorin: We only get ten dollars each, and not from Mitica, from one of his men, the guy who gave us the job.

Radu: Maybe you only get ten, 'cause you're a parasite. Bogdan talked to Mitica on the phone this afternoon and he said he's gonna give me fifty dollars.

Sorin: He was on the phone to Mitica?

Radu: Yeah, what are you gawking at? Bogdan can talk to that policeman whenever he wants.

Sorin: Guys like us never get to talk to Mitica.

Radu: Fuck him! Why did I get into all this shit? Why didn't I just stay in front of the telly, get a good sleep, be in shape for my tennis game?

Sorin: Stop shouting, you're waking up the dogs!

Radu: (*Grabs the package*) I have to see what Bogdan got me into!

Sorin: You can't!

(*Radu and Sorin are fighting for the package. Dogs start barking*)

Sorin: You woke up the dogs, Grandad!

Radu: (*Slaps him*) Didn't I tell you not to call me 'Grandad'?

Sorin: (*Gives up*) The dogs are coming for us!

Radu: They must have smelt a parasite somewhere.

Someone is screaming, setting on the dogs. The sound of a car engine. Radu and Sorin hide. A car full of people who scream and whistle passes.

Sorin: The Mad Dogs! Did you see them? It was the Mad Dogs!

Radu: What Mad dogs?

Sorin: They're drunk and they're going for the old Food Complex.

Radu: What do I care about those piss heads?

Sorin: They're destroying my Food Complex! I better get the hose! (*Runs away*)

Radu: And the package? What about the package? Sorin! If you go, I'll tell Mitica and he won't give you any money! You parasite! (*Runs after him*) I'm throwing your package down the drain and I'm off to the whores! You hear me? I'm throwing it!

SCENE 4: The basement of an old deserted food store

Bogdan: Are you gonna cover for me?

Sorin: I …

Bogdan: Even if Mitica pulls your toenails out? …

Sorin: Even …

Bogdan: Bullshit! You're gonna shop me before I'm even across the border.

Sorin: Have you seen a red helmet?

Bogdan: Fuck that! Tell me you're gonna cover for me!

Sorin: When?

Bogdan: Tomorrow night. I made a deal with a truck driver to take me to Germany. I'm gonna pay him when I get there.

Sorin: Why Germany and not … Sweden?

Bogdan: I heard you can make loads of money in Germany.

Sorin: You heard … And who's gonna give you the money to pay the driver?

Bogdan: Mitica's packages must be full of dollars. You can feel it when you press them, it has to be! … I'm sure that tomorrow night there'll be at least twenty thousand bucks in there.

Sorin: What if it's drugs?

Bogdan: Mitica wouldn't let us carry drugs.

Sorin: No but he'd leave us twenty thousand dollars? … See if there's a red helmet over there …

Bogdan: Fuck your red helmet! Are you gonna cover for me?

Sorin: (*Jumps*) Did you hear that? They've broken into the Store!

(*Sorin pulls a hose from under the pipes*)

Bogdan: If you don't cover for me, I'll tell them you asked me to steal their packages.

Sorin: Out of the way! *He connects one end of the hose to a water pump and turns on the tap.*

Bogdan: You are such a 'loser'! I'm gonna run away to Germany and …

Sorin: Listen, dick head! I've been hearing the same story for twenty-five years! The first person I heard this from was this guy in school, he used to listen to 'Free Europe'. He kept bragging about running away to Germany and how cool it was gonna be there, until one day, I told him to shut up and get the finger out. So he ran away and they shot him at the border. Since then, I keep hearing the same thing – 'I'm going, I'm sick and tired, fuck this country, I'll clean their toilets, but at least I'll be free!' Go, then, just go! But why tell me about it?

Bogdan: To get courage.

Sorin: After '89, Octavian, Daniel, Horia, Cornel, Andrei, Leonard, all my friends went abroad on work contracts: 'I'm going, Sorin, I'm going there to fulfil myself.' They told me that and they left … Never came back. But not one of them ever said to me: come on Sorin, come to Germany and earn a living!

Bogdan: Well, come with me, Sorin, come tomorrow night, come to Germany!

Sorin: No thanks, I'm busy.

Bogdan: Then spare me the moralizing! You're a loser! You keep whining, just like Dad. You both keep talking about the communists, the 'securitate' and that shitty regime that destroyed your lives. If you were smart enough and you were following your goal, you could have made it, even in the old days. Today is different, you have opportunities, freedom, all the chances you need and if you don't take advantage of them you're just a sap.

Sorin: Ah, just go off and live with the Krauts and stop annoying people here then.

Bogdan: You're afraid of escaping, Sorin, that's why you're not running. And even if someone gave you the courage, like that, overnight, you still wouldn't go, because there's no one would have you.

We hear Radu's voice: 'Sorin! Sorin!'

Bogdan: My Father! You told me he was going home after you finished the job!

Sorin: There's the red helmet! Behind you, on the pipe!

Bogdan: Turn off the light! ... Turn off the light when I tell you! (*Hits the bulb*)

Sorin: (*Turning on a flashlight*) You owe me a bulb.

Bogdan: Get rid of him! ... Send him away, quickly!

Sorin: What will you give me if I do?

Bogdan: Anything you want!

Sorin: Your Father.

Bogdan: My Father? ... What do you need him for?

Sorin: I need him for a week.

Bogdan: What about the packages?

Sorin: We're gonna make the deliveries.

Bogdan: On one condition – after a week, I'm gonna take Mitica's packages and run off to Germany!

Sorin: It's gonna cost you fifty dollars.

Bogdan: What?

Sorin: Taking care of your Father.

Bogdan: That's crazy money.

Radu's voice – 'Sorin, are you here?'

Bogdan: Deal – fifty dollars!

Sorin: Money first.

Bogdan: I don't have it on me, I'll give it to you tomorrow.

Radu's voice, very close – 'Sorin?'

Bogdan: Ok, fuck you, here's the money! If you take him to the whores I'll kick your arse!

Sorin: (*Takes the money*) Hey, Radu, get out of the way or I'll spray you with canal water! *Starts running, pulling the hose.*

Radu: (*Following him*) Where the hell were you, I've been looking for you …

SCENE 5: The old Food Complex

Sorin and Radu are waiting, on top of a wardrobe. Sorin is holding the hose, ready to turn on the water. Radu is playing with the flashlight.

Radu: I'm going down for a minute, to stretch my legs.

Sorin: Not now, we have to be ready when they come.

Radu: They're obviously not coming.

Sorin: They probably stopped for a drink on the way.

Radu: Come on, this isn't a Sergiu Nicolaescu movie! Who do you think you are? Detective Moldovan? I can't do this, I'm going for a slash …

Sorin: There, look, something moved! Turn on the flashlight!

Radu: There's nothing there, Sorin.

Sorin: It moved!

Radu: Hands up, Mad Dogs, or we're gonna spray you with shit!

Sorin: Shine the light on them!

Radu: It's only a dog. Stupid dog! Look at him, taking a piss. Why don't you spray him, he's pissing all over the cheese section.

Sorin: Those were the oil and vinegar shelves.

Radu: (*Nostalgically*) The prices in those days! … 5 lei for a bottle of sun-flower oil.

Sorin: No, it was 7 lei.

Radu: Excuse me, when I married my first wife, in '75, it was 5 lei.

Sorin: Don't you tell me what used to be in my store! There, that's where they kept the oil bottles from Constanta and Targoviste! (*Jumps down and moves through the imaginary shelves*) On this shelf – flour, 4 lei a kilo, maize, 8 lei a kilo, and there, pasta. On the other side, tins, pork liver, 4 lei, sardines, in oil or tomato, 9 lei a tin, and there, right where you're standing, used to be the fridge …

Radu: This was a fridge?

Sorin: Full of smoked rashers, 11 lei a kilo, pork fillet, 25 lei a kilo …

Radu: Listen, don't tell me what food you could find back in '75. Tell me what I could afford to eat now, with my seventh grade worker's salary.

Sorin: (*Like in a trance*) And then the crisis came and all the shelves were filled with tinned beans and jars of vegetables. My Mother used to hear the cheese truck coming. She'd shout from the kitchen: 'The cheese is coming, Sorin!' And I'd jump out of my room, bare-foot, running to this place, stopping here, in front of the stand, the stand was right here! And I was the first … No, the second or maybe third, but it didn't matter, because I was definitely gonna get cheese. I had to tell the other people in the queue that I was also queuing up for Octavian, Daniel, Horia, Cornel, Andrei's Mother, Leonard's Grandmother. Six people, plus my Mother, seven! Please don't push, make way, Cornel is here, there's Andrei's Mother! Come here, please make way, please! Stay in the queue, no cheating, please! Get in line, there's enough for everyone, yeah, cheese, 17 lei a kilo …

Radu: The car is here!

Sorin: With cheese?

Radu: The car with the Mad Dogs, you stupid parasite!

We hear the car braking. Sorin jumps on top of the ancient fridge and prepares the hose. Voices, shouts, music from a stereo.

Radu: Are you sure your water pump is working?

Sorin: It's a 1000 Watt pump. I installed it myself, piece by piece and then I connected it to the toilet pipe.

Radu: What type of weld did you use?

Sorin: Six millimetres.

Radu: And it works?

Sorin: I've been spraying the Mad Dogs for four months and they still won't give up.

Radu: If you want to spray water even ten meters you're gonna need a 2000 watt pump ... We'd better call the police to arrest those wankers. I know some guys in the special forces. They thought I was a terrorist.

Sorin: Are you scared?

Radu: You know, I found number 253 on that street. I rang and handed them the package with my eyes shut. That's why I came after you, to tell you not to worry. Now you can spray them.

Sorin: Thank you, Radu.

Radu: I like you, because you haven't forgotten. I haven't forgotten either. How could I, it's my life! I was happy back then. Were you?

Sorin: A parasite is always happy.

Radu: If we could only crack those idiots' heads open and stuff in everything we've suffered, they wouldn't come to destroy the Complex.

Sorin: I have a special nozzle. Keep the light on them!

The Mad Dogs come in. Five young men carrying bats and bottles of vodka. They drink and smash everything in their way.

Radu: 'Put your hands up punks, nobody moves! This is detective Moldovan from the Department of Justice!'

The Mad dogs don't seem to be bothered.

Sorin: Put the light on them and shut the fuck up!

Radu: 'Hands up, Semaca! You too, Lastarica! Not so fast. I'm detective Moldovan and you are all under arrest! Face the wall, reach for the sky! Spread 'em.'

Mad Dog 1: Blow me, stupid cop!

Sorin: (*Pointing the hose to them, like a machine gun*) I'll blow you, all right!

SCENE 6: Radu's apartment

Radu: He put the hose into the guy's mouth and the water came out of his ears, like a fountain …

Roxana: Did Bogdan take you to a horror movie again?

Radu: I tell you, if he'd had a 2000 Watt pump, the water would have come out the guy's arse.

Roxana: Couldn't you find something more interesting to do?

Radu: Then the second guy came at us with a bat, the fucking idiot! He kept screaming like the barbarians in that movie 'Columna'. Only he was a skin head. Which suited us. Sorin pointed the hose to the guy's head and almost put a hole in it.

Roxana: Radu, please!

Radu: Honestly, when the jet struck his head, the jet was as thick as my hand, it threw him against the wall! He was stuck to the wall, facing us, dazed and dripping. Then, Sorin sprayed him again, right in the chest. And Roxi, I'm telling you, those Mad Dogs are very well fed, big strong chests, not scrawny like Ionut and Bogdan. And the third one, we got him when he was running away, right in the back of the head …

Roxana: Stop it!

Radu: Why? It's exactly what happened.

Roxana: You fell in a ditch.

Radu: He sprayed me too, the hose isn't exactly perfect. I'll have to get some tools from work and fix it …

Roxana: Your shirt is a mess.

Radu: They were lucky in the end, I missed one of them, couldn't get the light on him. It was him carried the others to the car. The Mad Dogs have a 'Jeep'! Now, can you tell me how those shitheads can afford a car like that?

Roxana: Where did you steal the flour and the sugar from? And the rice? And the maize?

Radu: I took them from the Complex. Sorin took some too, less than me, of course, he doesn't have a family. And he gave the rest of it to the pensioners who live in his building. I gave the taxi driver five kilos of rice, three of flour and three of sugar, because I couldn't pay the fare.

Roxana: Did you see the sell-by date on this flour? And the rice? And the maize?

Radu: What's wrong with my flour? What's the problem? You're never happy! I brought you 30 kilos of flour and rice.

You can give some to your Mother and all the other greedy bastards in your family!

Roxana: Radu!

Radu: I can't say anything without you contradicting me!

Roxana: Have a look at what's written on the bags! Look. They're old, they're expired. Not by a month or two, sixteen years old! Did you see the sell-by date? 'November 1986'!

Radu: So what?

Roxana: I won't give food to Ionut that's older than he is!

Radu: I boiled some of the rice with Sorin and we ate it. And there's nothing wrong with me, I don't feel sick, no rashes, nothing! Same with the flour, the maize, the sugar, it's fresher than anything sold by those bastards in the local market.

Roxana: Where did you steal them?

Radu: Roxi, my sunshine, my water lily, my little pigeon, after we sprayed the Mad Dogs, we suddenly saw this shelf full of flour, only 4 lei a kilo. Do you remember the prices before '89? Even Sorin got scared. Where did it come from? Maybe the Mad Dogs brought it? But they only destroy things. I took as much as I could, actually I emptied the shelf …

Someone is flushing the toilet.

Roxana: Ionut is awake!

Radu: I'll go to him. (*Leaves*)

(*Roxana starts crying. She gets up and takes Radu's wallet from his trousers. It's empty. She starts crying again. Radu enters*)

Radu: Why is my butterfly crying?

Roxana: I don't know what to do with Ionut, I've taken him to every doctor available and now I can't afford his pills. And you're out every night with all kinds of idiots.

Radu: Why don't you take 20 kilos of the flour. Go to the best doctor there is and get a prescription for the kid. And don't let him sleep in the afternoon, he's a big boy now …

Roxana: Liar! You liar, with all your bloody flour and your bloody sugar!

Radu: I'm telling you the truth. After we sprayed them it just appeared, there it was.

Roxana: I must be stupid! Sitting here, listening to this bullshit!

Radu: Yeah, you are stupid for not trusting me!

Roxana: You're calling me stupid too?

Radu: Why, who else did?

Roxana: What are you calling me stupid for? For washing your clothes, for cooking your food, for being a slave in your house, because I had a child when you took me here. Is this what I deserve?

Radu: Okay, okay! I confess! I was fixing Bogdan's fridge, we had a couple of beers and I fell asleep in his house.

Roxana: And the flour? And the rice?

Radu: Well … they're from the European Union! Humanitarian aid. I was just passing through the market and they were unloading the trucks. I waited in a queue and I got lucky. Happy now? It's there in the paper, the Union has sent us help.

Roxana: Humanitarian aid. From 1986? Radu, stop making a fool of me!

Radu: Other people are making a fool of you, but you don't see that, 'cause you're too stupid! (*Leaves, slamming the door*)

SCENE 7: In the Supermarket

Radu has caught one of the Mad Dogs. Sorin is pointing the flashlight at him.

Radu: Now say 'Our Father', you stupid little shit, or I'll pump you full of water!

Sorin: Don't provoke him, he's violent!

Radu: Get your hands up punk, I gonna frisk you! (*Searches through his pockets and finds a penknife*) Well what do we have here? Look, Sorin, a gun! (*To the Mad Dog*) Hope you're thirsty punk, now open wide!

Sorin: Leave him, he's had enough!

Radu: What do you want with a knife, you parasite? What're ya, too good to work for a living like the rest of us? Where'd you get that 'Jeep'? Did your daddy give it to you, as a present? Who's your father? Some oil baron? A smuggler? You leeches are bleeding this country dry!

Mad Dog: I don't have a father, you moron!

Radu: A moron? (*To Sorin*) Did you hear that, he called me a moron! (*To the Mad Dog*) So you're the terrorist that's planting the bombs in the square! The one the police are after! Take your clothes off! Body search!

Mad Dog: Kiss my arse, Grandad!

Radu: (*Putting the hose into the guy's mouth*) I'll smash your teeth, you filthy parasite!

Sorin jumps and tries to stop Radu. They are fighting for the hose.

Mad Dog: (*Running out of the supermarket*) Fuck you, you morons! Fuck both of you!

Radu: (*Pulling the hose after him*) Just you wait, you fucking parasite!

Alone, Sorin starts searching through the supermarket. We hear Radu's voice: 'Get a job, you lazy bastards!' People shouting and whistling. Radu returns.

Radu: A lighter! Give me a lighter, I want to blow up their Jeep!

Sorin: That's enough, thank God they left!

Radu: They're sitting out there in the car like a bunch of pansies holding each others dicks, waiting for waterboy to come back. He's probably the only one who can drive. Give me a lighter, I want to set fire to their jeep, blow the shit out of it!

Sorin: We can't kill them or even cripple them!

Radu: Shit! I'm so stupid! I'll fill their petrol tank with water!

Sorin: Radu, they might attack you with their knives!

Radu: I'll fight back with this penknife, those punks don't scare me! *Leaves.*

Sorin goes down to the basement. We hear people screaming, then the car engine starting. Sorin comes back and continues inspecting the store. Radu enters.

Radu: The water stopped! It stopped, right after I put the hose inside the tank.

Sorin: Never touch my hose again! You broke the rules.

Radu: Whose rules?

Sorin: Mine. I'm not a criminal. I'm not a thug, like them. I'm just defending the Food Complex. I never attack or humiliate anyone. You hate them. Why are you so aggressive with a bunch of kids who don't know any better.

Radu: Oh, come on, you pump them full of dirty water, and now you're tortured with remorse?

Sorin: Leave!

Radu: Do you think it's easy for me to accept that I'm old and still poor? Those rich bastards encourage their kids to act like mad dogs. Giving them money for drugs and drink. That's why I am so angry, you know? … Years ago, I was a good person, ask Bogdan, I never laid a hand on him. Being poor made me bad, being poor and these times that I don't understand … I brought some tools to fix your hose, you can fix it yourself. *Leaves.*

Sorin winds up the hose. Something moves near the old fridge. Sorin grabs the hose, ready to fight. He realizes that the water pump has stopped.

Sorin: Radu! Radu!

Tries to run out of the supermarket, but the sounds coming from the fridge are growing in intensity. He is paralysed with fear.

Radu: (*Hidden, nearby*) I'm here, my friend!

Sorin: Turn on the pump!

Radu makes a sign that everything's ok and points in the direction of the sounds. Sorin throws him the flashlight and gets the hose ready. They both look like soldiers preparing for an assault. On Radu's signal, they attack the fridge.

Radu: Surrender! You're surrounded! *Imitates the sound of the police siren.*

Sorin: Shine the light!

A dog barking and then yelping.

Radu: Fucking dog, Jesus, he scared the shit out of me! (*Chases the dog*) Hey, why don't we train a couple of dogs to guard the store?

Sorin: I tried, but the Mad Dogs poisoned them.

Radu: See, and you tell me that they are only innocent kids. (*To the dog, who keeps sniffing something*) Don't worry about those bastards, little one, we took care of them!

Sorin: No, he smelt something else … They used to keep the meat in this old fridge.

Radu: Are you thinking what I'm thinking?

They touch the doors of the fridge with their hands.

Sorin: It's hot.

Radu: And moist.

They suddenly open the doors of the fridge. Pieces of meat are hanging on hooks.

Sorin: Pork carcasses!

Radu: Where's the cold air coming from, there's no ice, no motor, no electricity?

Sorin: Pork, pork carcass, 22 lei a kilo! Do you remember, Radu?

Radu: I remember, when I was young, they were 16 lei a kilo.

Sorin: (*In trance again*) My Mother woke me up at four o'clock in the morning. We went downstairs and we sat on the path, behind the Food Complex, dozing with our heads on our knees, until the queue started to form. By five o'clock, there were ten maybe fifteen people. We didn't care, me and my Mother were at the top. At half five, the head of the complex showed up and opened the butchers: 'I'm gonna call the abattoir and see if the meat truck is coming today.' He lied to us, but we knew it was coming, we were sure of that, that's why we didn't lose our courage. My Mother went home to put on another cardigan …

Radu: Come on, don't bore me with your queue saga! Jesus, I waited in plenty of queues myself in those days! Take a look at all this meat! There must be … (*counting*) twenty-five carcasses! Call your Mother and we'll cut a nice fillet for her!

Sorin: I'm not in the mood right now to tell you how my Mother died!

Radu: Oh, sorry! My first wife died too … This meat has me all emotional. I can't take it home because my fridge isn't big enough and Roxana will think I stole it anyway. Let's find a pair of scales and sell it in the street, quickly before it rots. We'll sell it cheap, undercut Nicu the butcher.

Sorin: We don't have a licence, the police would arrest us. We'll just give it to the people, like we did with the flour. (*Goes out in the street and shouts*) Meat! We have meat! The meat is here! The meat truck is here!

Radu: Save your breath, they're still asleep.

Sorin: Meat, meat, we have meat!

A pensioner shows up.

Pensioner 1: What kind of meat?

Radu: Pork. It's cheaper than Nicu the butcher's.

Sorin and Radu are improvising a market stall.

Sorin: It's free, you don't need any money.

Radu: Free my arse! Let me do the talking!

Pensioner 1: This meat's older than I am. Where did you steal it?

Radu: What the hell are you talking about? It's aid, from the European Union! It's all over the papers. (*Cuts a piece of meat with the penknife*) Smell it, if that's off I'll eat it raw!

Pensioner 1: (*Sniffing*) The European Union you say?

Sorin: Free!

Radu: That's the rule with this aid package, it has to be free.

Pensioner 1: I'll take five kilos! No, better give me ten!

Sorin: (*To Radu*) Cut a big piece for the gentleman!

Radu: (*Cutting*) Come on, people, meat from the European Union! Quality meat, meeting all European standards!

Sorin: (*To the people*) Please, form the queue on this side, don't push, there's plenty for everyone.

Radu: Come on, taste the pigs of the Union! (*Gives the pensioner his meat*) Sorin, I need some paper to wrap the meat, we can't hand it out like this. And a sharper knife, this one's blunt as … (*Enlightened*) Hey, this is my old penknife that the police confiscated! How did it end up in that Mad Dog's pocket?

Pensioner 2: Come on, hurry up with the meat!

Radu keeps serving. Sorin makes sure that everyone is queuing properly.

ACT II

SCENE 1: Radu's apartment

Bogdan: Smile! ... Now welcome the customer!

Roxana: (*Playing along badly*) Good day to you, sir! Can I help you? ... Are you familiar with our new shower gels?

Bogdan: Brands, Roxana! 'New shower gel brands' – that's how you address the customer, like a professional. Because he's buying a brand, not a sack of potatoes or fithy second-hand clothes.

Roxana: But why should I approach the customer in the first place? Why should I disturb him and burst into his life like that? Let him choose whatever he likes! If he were blind, then, I'd understand, I'd help him!

Bogdan: Because you have to sell! Don't you get it, Roxana? Sell! You, as a Head of a Department, are responsible for the sales volume. You're the one who gets burned if targets aren't reached. Smile! ... Welcome the client!

Roxana: But I've never used shower gel! How can I recommend shower gel to a man if I've never tried it?

Bogdan: Look, do this right and you'll be swimming in shower gel, lady of the lather, queen of the bubble bath. Just, smile!

Roxana: (*Lamentably*) Good day to you, sir! ...

Bogdan: You're grinning like an idiot.

Roxana: If it's not good enough find another Head of Department!

Bogdan: Roxana, smile naturally, a smile costs nothing! 'A "conquering" smile increases sales by a mile.' The customer's happy, he feels good, he likes you, buys your gel and he'll keep coming back, to you!

Roxana: What if he's hitting on me?

Bogdan: Shine, be chirpy, be happy that he came in to your shop and you can help him to choose, making him just as happy. Smile like it's your first date.

Roxana: Don't you get it? I can't smile like a teenager. (*Starts crying*) Stop pushing me, I can't! I can't laugh, I can't smile … I'm an old woman, Bogdan! Find a young one, one who knows what the hell shower gel is …

Bogdan: Do you realize what you're doing, Roxana? You're missing the biggest chance of your life because of a stupid smile.

Pause

Roxana: I'm late.

Bogdan: What?

Roxana: I haven't had my period yet.

Pause

Bogdan: … Oh, Jesus.

Roxana: It's his, don't worry.

Bogdan: Bullshit. You don't even remember the last time he got up on you.

Roxana: Your Mother got up on him, to have you!

Bogdan: If you say one more word about my Mother …

Radu's voice, accompanied by a violin, from the street: 'In front of the little house, there are so many flowers …'

Roxana: Radu! It's Radu!

Bogdan: You told me he wasn't coming until this afternoon!

Roxana: (*Runs to the window*) He's brought a gypsy band!

Opens the window and makes a sign. Radu's voice: 'But the most beautiful flower that I know, is you …' Roxana is laughing.

Bogdan: Close that window, you stupid woman!

Roxana: Yes, I am stupid, I'm stupid to take all this shit from you.

Bogdan: Save me the lecture! Where is he?

Roxana: Relax! He's just come into the building.

Bogdan is trying to jump off the window.

Roxana: The neighbours will see you!

Bogdan: I'll hide up on the top floor 'til he comes in.

Roxana: Are you too embarrassed to see your own Father?

Radu comes in followed by a violin player and a guitar player. He's wearing Sorin's red helmet on his head. He's holding a large bouquet of tulips in one hand and a plastic bag full of bottles in the other.

Radu: (*Sings*) 'Tell me now, beautiful Zaraza, who's the one who loves you …'

Falls down on his knees and hands Roxana the flowers. She accepts them and they sing together: 'How many people cried for you, and how many died …' They dance together. Roxana seems happy.

Radu: (*To Bogdan*) What are you doing sitting there like a twit, bring over some glasses and open a bottle of wine, the '75 Cotnari.

Roxana: I'll bring them!

Radu: No, you sit here, my love, I want you to have some fun! (*To Bogdan*) Here, a bottle of Pinot Noir, Odobesti, '81, and Busuioaca de Bohotin, '83 … (*To the gypsies*) Maestro, 'Tulips, tulips …'

Party atmosphere. Bogdan leaves the room. Radu and Roxana are singing 'Tulips, tulips …' Bogdan is back. He opens a bottle and fills the glasses.

Radu: A toast! To the love that binds all people together and to world peace!

Roxana: To love!

Everyone but Bogdan empties his glass.

Radu: What's the matter, Bogdan, got the shits again?

Bogdan: I feel sick.

Radu: Maestro, play something he likes, something to calm his stomach. What about that one, the one that those two blondes on the telly sing with the big knockers?

Roxana: Why don't you have a drink?

Bogdan: I won't drink that crap.

Radu: The whole quarter's drinking it: Biborteni and Borsec, mineral water, 3.50, including the bottle for everyone who still remembers the bad old days and wine, 12 lei a bottle. The shelves were emptied in an hour. Yesterday I had three boxes full of 'Amigo', instant coffee, three boxes, that's all they gave us …

Roxana: Expired: 1988.

Radu: Nobody died from my coffee yet, pumpkin. (*To Bogdan*) What are you staring at?

Roxana: Can't he look at his Father? He hasn't seen you in ages.

Radu: You don't now how to enjoy yourself, Bogdan! You don't drink, you don't dance, you don't go out with women. I pray for the day you introduce me to some nice girl you met.

Roxana: His time will come.

Bogdan: (*To Radu*) You're pathetic.

Radu: Well thank God you're so perfect!

Bogdan: You're making a fool of yourself going around like Romeo's grandad, croaking out that cheap flowery crap.

Radu: That's pure poetry, you ignoramus!

Bogdan: Did you sing them to my Mother too?

Roxana: Bogdan!

Radu: Yes, I did, because I loved her too!

Bogdan: Yeah, sure, that's why she ran away. Nobody believes your bullshit, Dad!

Roxana: I do!

Radu: How dare you judge me? I was the one wiped your arse. Your Mother was off in Germany in her museums and libraries. She forgot she had a baby back home. Am I guilty because she stayed there? Am I guilty because a drunken Kraut ran over her in his car?

Bogdan: You haven't lifted a finger to bring her home or bury her!

Roxana: Can't you understand? In those days, there was no way to bring back a defector's body?

Bogdan: No, he could've done it, only he was too much of a fucking coward. Now he's all pals with that tosser, Sorin Petric, he's even wearing that stupid helmet …

Radu: I got it for fixing his pump.

Bogdan: And you pretend to be the people's saviour with Mitica's money!

Radu: If I ever catch you doing his dirty little jobs again … Instead of going to University …

Bogdan: You seem to be doing okay since you took over those dirty little jobs …

Radu: What dirty jobs? I only did it once, when you sent me to 253 Baraj street. And you haven't even given me the fifty dollars, you promised me …

Bogdan: And you've never done another job since?

Radu: No! Because I discovered what it is to give for a change and that cured me of hatred, envy and malice. You have no idea what it feels like to give a piece of bread and ask for nothing in return. I gave them butter, and sausages, and cheese, a little bit of everything, whatever we found in the supermarket.

Bogdan: Jesus, you're such an arsehole!

Radu jumps up, ready to strike Bogdan.

Roxana: (*Defending him*) Don't hit him!

Radu: (*Takes out the penknife*) Remember this, Bogdan? You stuck it right into my heart.

Roxana: (*To the gypsies*) Please leave now, this party is over!

Radu: I say when the party is over! (*Drinks*) Maestro! (*Sings*) 'Only my heart knows, how dear you are to me …'

Bogdan leaves, Roxana follows him. Radu lies down on the bed, drinking and singing: 'Who could understand our love and the way we trembled …'

SCENE 2: The supermarket

Bogdan: Finders keepers!

Sorin: You don't even know how to turn on the pump.

Bogdan: (*Unwinding the hose and pointing it to Sorin*) Are you fucking with me, 'loser'?

They hear a car engine.

Sorin: The Mad Dogs!

Bogdan: Your pump was stuck, my friend, so I thought I'd get you a tanker. Only I couldn't find a tanker full of dirty water. Sorry about that, they only had petrol, five thousand litres of petrol.

Throws down the flashlight and lights a match. Roxana comes in.

Roxana: You're gonna have petrol coming out your ears, like a fountain.

Sorin: Why, Bogdan?

Bogdan: Punishment, for not delivering Mitica's packages, like we agreed.

Sorin: I took care of your Father. Kept him from the whores.

Roxana: Stay away from my husband!

Bogdan: Shut up! Give me that package you never delivered. Remember, 253 Baraj Street!

Roxana: And what about that depot you stole that old food from!

Bogdan: Give me the package and Mitica will forget this ever happened, just don't show your face around here again.

Sorin: You're in this with Mitica?

Bogdan: The City Council's gonna auction this place. Mitica's going to bid whatever it takes.

Sorin: When's the auction?

Bogdan: None of your business!

Roxana: Our house stinks with rotten food and it's all your fault. Radu goes on and on about the prices in the old days. That's why we never make any progress in this country like the Americans or the Germans. There's too many nostalgic people here, like you two! You should all be sent to – China!

Sorin: Can I take my pump?

Bogdan: The Mad Dogs are going to throw it in the dump. Mitica's paying them to do up the supermarket. And you, like an idiot, spraying them. Now, I want that package and I want it now!

Sorin: When you get to Germany, you're gonna write to us every day, because letters are cheaper than phone calls. You'll send us long letters describing the streets, the shops, the houses, what life is like there. The joy of writing will make you forget for a while the worry of finding a black market job, and the fear that the money stolen from Mitica will slowly run out or the terror that the Germans might catch you and send you back …

Roxana: What's he talking about, Bogdan?

Sorin: You'll keep writing until you find a job. Then you'll send us postcards, 'Wishing you a Happy New Year!' (*to Roxana*) I'm sure you'll be delighted to get a Christmas card with the Brandenburg Gate on it.

Roxana: You're going to Germany, Bogdan?

Sorin: He's not going, he's running away with Mitica's money.

Bogdan: That loser is bullshitting you! I'm putting you in charge of a whole department. I'll teach you how to organize promotions for shower gel with competitions and prizes. Look, right here, we'll have a stand with all the shower-gel brands, '15 % discount'. And the big prize will be … Roxana, are you paying attention? The big prize will be …

Roxana: A trip to Germany! *Runs off.*

Bogdan: Roxana, don't listen to him! (*Threatens Sorin with the hose*) Where's that package?

Sorin: There's 20,000 dollars in there, we split it 50/50.

Bogdan: I want 15,000, for trying to screw me. Come on, cough it up!

Sorin: I put it in the bank, 5,000 a lodgement, so's not to draw attention to it.

Pensioner 1 shows up.

Pensioner 1: Mister Sorin! Hey, mister, where are you?

Bogdan: I want my share by tomorrow night!

Sorin: The day after tomorrow.

Bogdan: If you try and screw me again you're dead! *Throws away the hose and runs out.*

Sorin: Please, come in, what can I do for you?

Pensioner 1: I knew I'd find you on duty. Mister Sorin, the People's Association in my building have sent me. We need some yoghurt and sour cream this morning.

Sorin: I'll let you know if we get some in.

Pensioner 1: Do you remember yoghurt and sour cream, 4 lei a bottle?

Sorin: The yoghurt bottle was blue, and a red bottle for the cream.

Pensioner 1: Back in '76, the shelves were full of yoghurt and cream. They were made from real milk, not like now, now they're full of chemicals to make them last longer. Can you get the European Union on the phone and ask them if we have to queue up?

Sorin: I'll let you know if something happens, sleep well!

Pensioner 1: If they send you some yoghurt, save four bottles for me, please. I'll look after you, don't worry. *Searches through his pockets.*

Sorin: No, please, you don't have to!

Pensioner 1: Come on, Mister, you scratch my back ... there's a good living in this aid business. What, did you think I wasn't going to notice your car out front?

Sorin: Ah, you mean the petrol tanker? (*We hear the tanker going away*)

Pensioner 1: Is that a tanker? Ok, I'll pretend I never saw it. But tell me, what do you do when it rains? Is there one of those roofs that pulls up?

Sorin: What roof? Where the hell did you see a convertible? *Goes out of the supermarket, looking for the car.*

Pensioner 1: Are you gonna save me some yoghurt? Call the EU, mister, tell them to send me four bottles, please! …

SCENE 3

In the middle of the supermarket, a convertible Jeep. Outside it's raining.

Radu: It's a trap, Sorin. They left the Jeep out in the open to trick us. Get the hose, I'll go start the pump.

Sorin: The Mad Dogs never attack the Complex when it's raining.

Radu: Are you sure? Maybe they stole the car, left it in here, thinking the police would arrest us.

Sorin: After '89, the Food Complex went bankrupt and the space was deserted for three years, until a car salesman took it. After six months, he went out of business.

Radu: Do you think it just appeared, out of the blue, like the flour and all the other things? …

Sorin: (*Pointing to the car*) Look, something's written here – 'Shower Gel' – Grand Prize!

Radu: It's our prize, Sorin! God sent it to us because we helped the poor. Let's sell the car and split the money!

Sorin: Who's gonna buy it with no registration or keys even?

Radu: We'll sell it to Mitica and make a packet. How much would a beauty like this go for?

Sorin: About 20,000 dollars.

Radu: I'm rich! I'll buy a three-room apartment and I'll rent out the old one. I'll buy a camel-hair overcoat for myself and a washing machine for Roxana, I'll send Ionut to a better school. A rich gentleman! And you too, Sorin! You can sit and do absolutely nothing, like a parasite.

Sorin: And the Food Complex?

Radu: Fuck the Food Complex! What, do you want to keep spraying those idiots until you die of rheumatism? Ok, I'll tell you what, if you ever miss the old pump, you can still come, every now and then and spray all you like.

Sorin: Ok, I'll sell you my share.

Radu: What do you mean?

Sorin: You give me 10,000 dollars and I help you push the car to your house. I pushed it in here all by myself, with the handbrake on.

Radu: Have you lost the plot completely?

Sorin: Okay, 8,000, and you'll get more from Mitica.

Radu: Sorin, my friend, where in the name of God would I get that kind of money?

Sorin: Look, Radu, 5,000, if you pay me right now.

Radu: You're not telling me something. There's something going on in that little head of yours that I don't know about and it's bothering me.

Sorin: You can pay me in instalments.

Radu: You want to know how much money I've saved my entire life? Zero. I have no money in the bank, Sorin. I'm broke, trust me. Or do you want to take a look at a statement?

Pensioner 1 appears.

Pensioner 1: Mister Sorin, did you get the yoghurt and cream that I asked you for?

Radu: What yoghurt?

Pensioner 1: I asked you to save four bottles from the EU.

Sorin: It's raining …

Radu: Flooding, flooding has held up delivery from the European Union. Please come back tomorrow.

Pensioner 1: But don't forget about me please, four bottles …

Radu: Four, I'm gonna put that on my list. (*To Sorin*) See, you got them used to free food?

Pensioner 1: Nice car you have there, mister Sorin.

Radu: Ooooops! Now you're a car owner, mister Sorin.

Sorin: I've already told you it's not mine. We'll donate it to an old folks home.

Radu: Will you please shut up! What's your problem, mister? Didn't I tell you already – we don't have any yoghurt.

Sorin: Get into the car, make yourself comfortable. Unfortunately, we can't give you a spin, we ran out of petrol.

Radu: Don't break anything in there! The price of that would pay your funeral expenses ten times over!

Pensioner 1: Oh, it's your car.

Radu: It's uh … Mr … Shower-Gel's car, did you ever hear of him?

Pensioner 1: The seats are soft, like an armchair.

Radu: This guy, Gel, is a famous businessman. He gave it to us to wash it … Wait! Don't move! Look straight at the wall in front of you! Are you looking?

Pensioner 1: I'm looking.

Radu: And what do you see?

Pensioner 1: The wall, what else?

Radu: (*To Sorin*) What does it look like?

Sorin: An old man driving a Jeep.

Radu: You're blind. It looks like Roxana watching soaps on the telly. (*To the pensioner*) Hey, you, what would you like to see right now on this blank wall?

Pensioner 1: I came for the yoghurt.

Radu: Tell me what you'd like to see!

Pensioner 1: I can't see anything, I feel sleepy, like I'm watching a film.

Radu: Did you hear that, Sorin? Like a film! Let's make a drive-in cinema, just like in America.

Sorin: It's stupid.

Radu: Why do you reject the will of the people? We clean the place up a bit, we put in recycling bins every four meters, we rent a projector, I ask Roxana to sew a few sheets together for the screen and we paint spaces on the ground for the cars, like in a car park. If they don't have a car, they can bring their own armchair, I don't care, as long as they pay in. And a shop, of course, with pop-corn and minerals!

Sorin: It can't be done.

Radu: Yes, it can! We put on American films in the evening, dirty movies with tits and filth at night, and for the matinees – we put on Romanian movies for pensioners.

Pensioner 1: And when do you put on the yoghurt?

Radu: Sorin, don't you miss a good old communist movie? Ones with prime-secretaries and model workers, and laughing your ass off seeing comrade welder and comrade factory girl, walking hand in hand in the park. And then shout …

Pensioner 1: (*Whistles*) Fuck her! Fuck her!

SCENE 4: Radu's apartment

Roxana: Get Out!

Sorin: Radu wants to know, if you could sew a couple of sheets together, as a screen, we need it for the opening of the cinema.

Roxana: Where's Radu?

Sorin: He's sleeping in the basement of the Food Complex.

Roxana: Why don't you let him sleep in his own house?

Sorin: We have to get the cinema open.

Roxana: Fuck you! Tell Radu, Ionut's in the hospital. If he doesn't come home this evening I'm gonna leave him.

Sorin: You won't be happy on your own.

Roxana: What the fuck do you care about my happiness? Get out!

Sorin: I can persuade him to give up the Food Complex for good.

Roxana: If Radu finds out anything about me, Bogdan will kill you.

Sorin: Radu hid the package we were supposed to take to 253. There's a lot of money in that package. If we give Mitica his money back, Bogdan won't have enough cash to go to Germany and leave you. Mitica will forgive Radu and me. He'll buy the supermarket and you'll become Head of Cosmetics.

Roxana: Why should I believe you?

Sorin: If you help me find the package, I'll give Radu my half of the Jeep.

Roxana: Where did you get a Jeep? Don't tell me, your uncle in America sent it to you? Come on, cut the shit, I'm not that stupid!

Sorin: It's a real car, it appeared in the supermarket two nights ago. You could sell it and buy a big three-room apartment. Radu'll buy you a washing machine.

Roxana: Swear you didn't steal it, like the food Radu brought me!

Sorin: I swear! Everything that we've found in the supermarket is because of Radu's faith. Every time he chased away the Mad Dogs, God sent him as a gift whatever he was thinking about.

Roxana: I'd love to play water games and get loads of money from God.

Sorin: Radu has suffered more than the rest of us.

Roxana: Him, an ordinary worker, who goes in every day to that stupid Institute? He didn't suffer during Ceausescu's time either. He watched the Revolution on TV from behind the couch. What has he suffered to deserve miracles?

Sorin: He believes in God. Do you?

Roxana: I don't know … I wish I could … but … I'm too tired for that.

Sorin: Let's find that package and tomorrow morning Radu will come back home.

Roxana: If I find it, do you swear to give it back to Mitica and never bother Radu again?

Sorin: I swear!

Roxana: On your Mother!

Sorin: (*In trance again*) My Mother? … My Mother went to get another cardigan. She was gone for half an hour. Then the meat truck arrived and the people formed a queue. I was the first, no, the second or third, but I was also queuing for Octavian, Daniel, Horia, Cornel, Andrei's Mother and Leonard's Grandmother. Six people, plus my Mother, seven! Please, don't push, there's plenty for everyone, the truck has just arrived, the administrator lied to us, but I knew the meat was coming! This is my Mother, she's been queuing since four o'clock this morning, she just went home to get another cardigan … But the people pushed her back: 'You haven't been queuing! We didn't see you!' 'Yes, she was, she was here with me, she's my Mother!' I cried, but the people called me a liar. I asked

Octavian, Daniel, Horia, Cornel, Andrei's Mother and Leonard's Grandmother to tell the people that my Mother had the right to join me in the queue. They didn't say a word. None of them. Their silence made my Mother very angry and she tried to force her way into the queue, to regain her place. But the people pushed her back again: 'Get back, get back to the back of the line, you cheat!' and my Mother fell down on the path. Right at our feet. Nobody helped her, nobody left the line, not even Octavian, or Daniel, or Cornel …

Roxana: But why?

Sorin: They would have lost their place in the queue for meat. My Mother had a heart attack.

Roxana: And you, why didn't you help her?

Sorin: I was on my way to the pay phone to call an ambulance.

Roxana: Bastards!

Sorin: Hunger and squalor have made us turn our backs on God. We're nothing but empty shells …

Five men wearing masks break into the apartment. They are carrying baseball bats. One of them attacks Sorin.

Roxana: (*To Sorin*) Don't be frightened, it has to be one of Bogdan's jokes! He paid the Mad Dogs to scare me …

Mad Dog 1 is hitting Roxana. The woman falls down unconscious. Sorin manages to break loose and jumps out the window.

Mad Dog 1: (*Stopping the man who was trying to follow Sorin*) Leave him! Go in the other room! (*To the other men*) Go search the bathroom and the kitchen!

SCENE 5: The supermarket

It's raining.

Voice 1: The meat truck is here!

Voice 2: Do they have pork?

Voice 3: Keep a place in the queue for me!

Voice 4: Keep a place for Octavian, Daniel, Horia and Cornel!

Radu: Sorin, is that you?

Voice 1: They've started selling!

Voice 2: Only one kilogram per person please, so we all get some!

Radu: Sorin, cut the shit, we should have started the film by now … Sorin, are you there?

Voice 3: Don't push! Go back to the back of the line, you cheat!

Voice 4: My son has kept a place for me!

Radu: Who's there?

Radu is caught by several flashlights. He tries to hide, but the lights follow him. He tries desperately to avoid them.

Voice 1: Why didn't you hold a place for me?

Voice 2: My poor children haven't eaten meat for a whole month!

Voice 3: That's your second time coming up to buy, you pig, have you no shame?

Voice 4: Is the cheese truck here yet?

Radu: Leave me alone! (*Crossing himself*) 'Our Father who art in Heaven …' (*He forgets*) …'Our Father who art in Heaven … Give us this day our daily bread …' Bloody hell! Why are you stirring up the past, you devil?

Voice 5: Traitor!

Radu: Traitor, me? I never betrayed anyone! I did what I had to do to get a little piece of meat from Nicu the butcher. I knew him from school. I slipped him some money, big deal. But I queued for eggs, for cheese … That's not treachery! I did what I had to do, like every other Romanian!

Voice 5: You snake in the grass, you weasel! You ratted on people and ate crap!

The Mad Dogs are surrounding Radu, threatening him with the bats. Radu is blinded by the flashlights.

Radu: Mercy! Have mercy! … I disowned my first wife when she defected to West Germany. I accused her in a public meeting of my fellow workers at the Optical Institute. That was back in '77. These are my sins, have mercy!

Voice 5: Confess everything, snitch!

Radu: If I hadn't accused her in a public meeting, the Party would have taken my apartment. What was I to do?

Voice 5: Spit it out!

Radu: I gave the Securitate Officers all the letters she sent me from West Germany.

Voice 1: Now say 'Our Father', you stupid little shit, or I'll pump you with water!

Radu: Is that you, parasite?

Mad Dog 1: Where's Mitica's package?

Radu: The package? I took it to Baraj Street …

Mad Dog 5: (*Hits him*) The package!

Radu: Sorin knows where the package is! He's got it! He's not here, he's gone to get the film. Sorin Petric has it …

(*Radu falls unconscious. The Mad Dogs leave. Silence. The stage is lit by neon lights. The old communist store is now a modern supermarket, with new shelves and refrigerators full of shining merchandise. In the middle of the supermarket – the Jeep and a stand full of shower gel bottles. Pensioner 1 turns up*)

Pensioner 1: Hey, mister, what are you doing? We're queueing up outside, and you're asleep in here? Is it nice to keep old customers waiting in the rain?

Radu: (*still dizzy*) The Mad Dogs never come when it's raining

Pensioner 1: The stuff has arrived, mister! Why don't you let us in?

Radu: Didn't I tell you already that I'll show Romanian movies at the matinee? Go get some sleep! … (*discovers the new surroundings*) My God, how did you do that?! It's a real supermarket, like in the American films!

Pensioner 1: (*to the people outside*) Aid from the Americans!

Pensioner 2: Open the store! Have you no shame, toying with us like this?

Radu: There is no aid! I'm giving nothing away for free! (*Pushing Pensioner 1*) Get a trolley and pay the cashier, if you want yoghurt! (*To the people outside*) This is a supermarket now, no more charity!

People shouting and whistling, windows broken. A bunch of people break inside and start taking everything they can get their hands on. Radu is

being manhandled and thrown to the floor. Voices: 'Aid! Humanitarian Aid from the Americans!'

SCENE 6: The supermarket

Shower gel bottles on the floor, around the Jeep.

Bogdan: Dad, what the hell are you doing here?

Radu: I gave out aid to everyone in the city. It was crazy: French cheese, tins of all colours and sizes, sausages, meat, meat, meat for all Romanians! European aid is no match for American aid. 'Made in the USA' boy!

Bogdan: Dad, you're so stupid! You're the most stupid creature on the planet!

Radu: Why? Because I raised you, worked for you, because I gave charity to the people?

Bogdan: That aid you gave to those morons was Mitica's stock! Mitica bought the supermarket yesterday in an auction. I've had people putting in shelves, fridges and everything all afternoon. And in the evening, the food trucks arrived. A hundred and fifty people have been working non-stop to get this supermarket opened by this morning. You've destroyed my work, Dad!

Radu: You don't know what work is …

Bogdan: I'm 'brand manager' in Mitica's supermarket! Do you get it, you stupid man?

Radu: That's bullshit! I've been working like a slave for the last two days to open a cinema here.

Bogdan: Well where were you yesterday afternoon?

Radu: Sleeping in the basement, I was exhausted after all that work.

Bogdan: Then you woke up, all ready to destroy Mitica's supermarket.

Radu: Bogdan, come on. Who's your Father? Me, or that scumbag cop Mitica?

Bogdan: I'm Mitica's son just as much as Sorin Petric is yours.

Radu: Are you jealous?

Bogdan: Your precious Sorin stormed into the auction rooms and tried to buy the supermarket. In your name. So, where did you get the money from, Dad?

Radu: That's rubbish! I sent him to the National Archives to get an old film.

Bogdan: Where's the package Dad?

Radu: I took it to the address, just like you said.

Bogdan: What did the guy who took the package look like?

Radu: I've no idea. I rang the bell and Sorin handed him the package. I kept my eyes shut, like you told me. Is there a problem?

Bogdan: You're lying! Your lies are so big they've reached the heavens! Even my Mother can hear them, old man!

Radu: Listen carefully, Bogdan. Your Mother can't hear me up there. I'm sorry but she can't because I had no faith. But the charity that I give to the people will bring me closer to God and the Heavens will open for me too.

Bogdan: Bullshit! I'm not interested in redemption! I've got responsibilities, Dad! I'm in business! I want power! …

Noises are coming from direction of the old refrigerator)

Bogdan: Is someone there?

Radu: Stray dogs.

Bogdan: There's no dogs! I made sure we got them all, a supermarket should be as clean as a hospital.

Radu: Maybe you missed one.

We hear the noises again.

Bogdan: Mister Mitica, is that you? It's Bogdan, the 'brand manager' of the supermarket.

Radu: Nobody's ever seen your Mitica, Bogdan!

Bogdan: Stay out of this! … Mister Mitica, I'm sorry, but something unexpected happened. I had everything in place: the products on the shelves, prices, discounts, the staff trained in, I even hired an orchestra to play the National Anthem. Everything was ready for you to cut the ribbon with the golden scissors and …

Someone is coughing near the fridge.

Bogdan: I assume full responsibility for this failure … It's all my fault, please forgive me, mister Mitica. Please! (*Falls down on his knees*) I promise to correct my mistake and in 24 hours you will be the owner of the most modern supermarket in town. And your package, I'll find your package as soon as possible, mister Mitica! I haven't stolen a single dollar from you …

Radu: Say the 'Our Father', Bogdan! … (*Towards the fridge*) Mister Mitica, this is Radu Onica! Can you hear me? The people say that you were a policeman in the old days and now you're in business, buying everyone off. The people are wicked. I don't believe them ... I have some bad news for you. I can't be bought. I don't know what your relationship with my son is, but this place is a cinema. It belongs to the people, and my associate and myself are running it ...

Pensioner 1 appears from behind the fridge. He's holding a bottle of yogurt and drinks from it.

Pensioner 1: When does the movie start, mister?

Radu: What the hell are you doing here? Who let you in? ... Bogdan, look, it's only one of my customers! (*Kisses the man*) What are you drinking there, old man?

Pensioner 1: Yoghurt! I got eight bottles, from the American aid ...

Bogdan: Get out! (*Pushing the man*) Out! Father, please stop fucking me around! Where is that package?

Radu: See, if you say the 'Our Father', your troubles disappear. Go to Mitica and teach him the 'Our Father', that'll protect him from all harm.

Bogdan: Ok ... I'll go and ask him to spare you, because you're my father. But only you.

Radu: I don't need that cop's forgiveness. It's your forgiveness I need, for never teaching you how to pray.

Bogdan: Look, I promise I'll play tennis with you, I'll even let you beat me, we'll go to the pub and sing Al Bano and Tom Jones songs.

Radu: And then you can make fun of me, and get the Mad Dogs to strip search me again!

Bogdan: Please leave this place. Just go. This is private property now. If you want to make some money, clean up the mess you and your friends made. And stack those bottles for the promotion we're trying to organize. Anyone who buys a bottle, gets a chance to win the grand prize – the Jeep!

Radu: That's my car and Sorin's!

Bogdan: None of this was yours, ever.

SCENE 7

People have gathered inside the supermarket.

Radu: Patience, 'Greetings From Agigea' will start in five minutes. You'll love it! Do you remember it? The young communists slaving like idiots on the Danube–Black Sea canal …

Pensioner 1: Any chance of some smoked bacon today?

Pensioner 2: And some Romanian chicken legs. The American ones are tasteless!

Radu: Tomorrow maybe, today is for having fun. Come on buy your tickets! Everyone who buys a ticket gets free shower-gel and is in with a chance to win the raffle. The big prize is 'The Shower Gel Jeep'!

Pensioner 3: You should get some coats and boots for us, it's nearly winter!

Pensioner 2: We don't care about films! We've no food and the price of medication goes up and up all the time. Boooooo! You dirty crook! We bought tickets for your film and you're giving us nothing in return?

Radu: I'm giving you Romanian films, so we can laugh about the old days!

Pensioner 1: I had to bribe you to get four bottles of yoghurt from the EU!

Radu: Who the fuck did you bribe, Grandad? You fucking liar!

Pensioner 1: You're a fucking liar! Treating an old man like that … I went to school in the fifties and in our schoolbook, when we had to learn the letter 'G', we were told that the Romanian soldier Gheorghe was fighting next to the Russian soldier Gherasim. They were both killing the Germans.

Radu: They would have been better off fighting against the guerillas in Guatemala.

People protesting, shouting and whistling. Sorin enters.

Sorin: Radu, please give up!

Radu: (*To the people*) The film is here! Sorin Petric is here with the film! (*to Sorin*) I only sold six tickets. Ask them to buy some more!

Sorin: We have to run!

Radu: Where's the film, you parasite?

Sorin: Mitica has sent the Mad Dogs to get the package back.

Radu: Why did you go to the auction? Did you try to buy the supermarket in my name? Now people will think I've been making a fortune stealing humanitarian aid …

Sorin: I was trying to save the old Food Complex. If I lose it, my life has no meaning. What did you do with the package, Radu?

The protests are gaining in intensity. The people verbally abuse Sorin and Radu.

Radu: (*Pointing to the Jeep*) Look, people, the car with the donations is here!

Pensioner 1: From where?

Radu: From NATO! We received dollars from NATO! If you queue up each of you will receive a 100 dollar bill.

Pensioner 2: Why a hundred?

Radu: So you can buy pills and pay the rent!

Pensioner 3: They have dollars from NATO!

People shouting, applauding. Radu goes inside the car. The people are forming a queue.

Radu: The car is here, Sorin! Wait in line and you'll get a few dollars for Mitica!

Sorin: (*In a trance*) And for Octavian, Daniel, Horia, Cornel, Andrei's Mother and Leonard's Grandmother …

Radu: If you keep pushing, you won't get any dollars! Do you want to embarrass us in front of NATO? Sorin, my boy, organize this queue, this is crazy!

Sorin: Please, make some order, everyone will keep his place! Don't push, there's plenty for everyone! Here, right after this gentleman is my place, I'm waiting for another six people!

Radu: (*Taking a package out of the red helmet*) The donations are here! Have a look, they're perfectly sealed, I won't have it said that I'm stealing donations!

People applauding.

Pensioner 2: Come on, hurry up with those donations!

Pensioner 1: They should only give fifty dollars, that way there'd be enough for everyone!

The Mad Dogs appear and start beating Sorin with the baseball bats.

Radu: Help! Help! The Mad Dogs are killing Sorin!

Nobody moves in the queue. Roxana enters.

Roxana: Radu, give them the money! Those psychos have destroyed our house!

Radu: (*He's trying to save Sorin but Roxana stops him*) Sorin, go to the pump, I'll get the hose!

Roxana: Stay out of this, Radu! I'm pregnant …

Radu: I'm gonna be a father?

Roxana: It's our baby!

The Mad Dogs keep hitting Sorin. Roxana takes the package from Radu and throws it to the Mad Dogs.

Roxana: Take your money and get out!

Pensioner 1: Our donations!

People pushing and running. The Mad Dogs take the package and leave. Some of the people are following them: 'Police! Stop the thieves! They stole the NATO donations!' Some of them are holding Radu responsible for the tragedy.

Radu: People, the Nato donations are here!

Pensioner 2: Are you blind? They stole them!

Roxana: Let's go home, Radu!

Radu: Be patient, petal! As soon as I finish giving out the donations, we'll take the Jeep and go to the movies. (*To the* *people*) We have the real NATO donations! (*Silence*) Those were fake, I put ordinary paper inside, just like American movies. Form a queue, I'll give you the donations in a second! Roxana, go to Sorin and take care of that parasite!

Radu goes down in the basement. The people are forming the queue silently.

Roxana: Don't die, parasite!

Sorin: If Octavian, Daniel, Horia, Cornel, Andrei come … If they come, tell them I saved a place in the queue for them … *Dies.*

We hear the siren of an Ambulance. Radu returns, pulling the hose, threatening the people who wait in line.

Radu: Now say 'Our Father', you stupid little fuckers, or I'll pump you full of water!

Stop the Tempo!

By Gianina Cărbunariu

Translated by Andrei Marinescu
Adapted by Paul Meade

Marius Ianus is the author of the poems included in the text.

(Collections: *The Anarchist Manifesto*; *The Bear In The Garbage Bin*, Vinea Publishing House)

Characters

Maria
Paula
Rolando

[**Maria**, **Paula** and **Rolando** are the names of the actors for whom this play was written. Each of the three characters in the play has a name, but does do not know the others' names. I used the names of the actors in order to differentiate the three voices and that's because they have been a source of inspiration to me, with their problems and thoughts.]

Setting: *Clubs, a car, etc. This play was designed to be performed in a club or similar space. The actors create all lighting effects using hand-held electric flashlights shining them on each other as necessary.*

SCENE 1

Loud music. Club lighting. Music and lights suddenly stop. Complete darkness. After a few minutes, enough to annoy people, Paula lights up a cigarette. It's a sign for Rolando who puts the light of the torch on her face. Paula takes a few drags of her cigarette then puts it out, looks at the audience, then:

Paula: Shit.

The following fragments could be performed mimicing different cultural genres. For example: TV advertisements, TV interviews, Chat shows, In the style of a DJ etc.

Rolando: You know now that I think about it, I didn't get a single phone call that whole month …

Paula: Shit.

Maria: This thing with the jobs was driving me crazy. Yeah, I couldn't believe that I was holding down three jobs at the same time. Seriously. I was so tired I couldn't even sleep at night.

Paula: Shit.

Rolando: I don't like using big words … in fact, I never use big words … like … I don't know … you know … like … anyway … I can't think of any … but back then, I was feeling like …

Paula: Shit.

Maria: Three jobs. And the hope that I'll get a place of my own. A cute little flat. A cute little husband. A cute little kid. A cute little car. A cute little crap.

Rolando: … Say it without big words … without big … big …

Maria: I'm only twenty-seven years old and I have three jobs … people I was in college with would have killed to be me. The only thing I had a slight problem with was fucking. But that was my little secret.

Paula: A piece of shit, that's what it was …

Rolando: I was tired. That's what it really was … And I couldn't get a gig. The clubs weren't calling anymore. I thought I wasn't good enough. 'I have to keep practising' – that's what I told myself. I have to take that vinyl and scratch all day long. (*Rolando speaks the following with a rhythm similar to a DJ scratching a record*) And I have to *be* cool. I have to *be* cool. I have to *be* cool. I have to *be* cool. I have to *be* cool. I have to *be* cool!

Maria: And then this asshole, the gynaecologist, said that at my age I should have a much more active sex life. Sex life? What sex life? I didn't have one because I was wasting my time working to pay the bills. Including his, the fucking asshole … So my sex life was …

Paula: Shit.

Rolando: I have to be cool. I have to be cool. You have to relax, you have to get outside of it … you have to have a few … if you have a smoke you're automatically cool, you have to chill out. No, you've got to freak out, you gotta dance, 'can you feel that, can you feel that, are you hearing it? C'mon, push the tempo, PUSH THE TEMPO! Push, push, push. It's like you're so fuckin' cool, man! C'mon!'

Paula: Shit.

Maria: In the end, I said to myself – what's wrong with dating your gynaecologist? I wasn't serious about him. You see I had the feeling he was married.

Rolando: Mmm. Hmmm.

Maria: Or recently divorced.

Rolando: Sure, sure.

Maria: Or God knows what.

Rolando: Yeah, right.

Maria: Yeah, because the first time we went out together he said something while discreetly touching my hand. He said something in English, I didn't know whether it was to impress me or to tell me something. And then he said, in a very serious voice, 'you understand, don't you?' The only thing I understood was 'I AM … and then something else, I'm not sure, because I was a bit tipsy and I had only started taking English lessons a month before that. Because I lied and said I could speak English for my third job. So I told him 'does it matter?' After all, what could have really mattered? …

Paula: A piece of shit.

Rolando: And the love of my life, well that month, a thirteen-year-old girl who looked like twenty-three. She had a thing for DJs. Her DJ obsession was so bad she broke up with me the minute I stopped getting gigs. So she left me for DJ Fucker or

DJ Big Dick or DJ Big Shit something like that. Someone who was more 'now' than me. And so more intensely cool.

Maria: We didn't see each other that often because … well … there was no point in asking him why. I wasn't interested anyway. And with all my jobs I had no time for that …

Paula: Shit.

Rolando: Yeah, I had to go clubbing. I had to be seen … in those days I think I even had a few fans … of course, if I think of it, it was bloody boring running around three or four clubs every night … but back then I guess I thought … that's the job.

Maria: Of course, I didn't feel like wasting my time in bars … of course I would have preferred to … but well, that was part of the game … and anyway, I can only sleep if I take a Xanax, so …

Rolando: So I grabbed a pair of …

Paula: Shit.

Maria: Because, if I want to, I could look really …

Rolando: …super-cool …

Maria: …like a lady …

Rolando: …extremely west …

Maria: …sexy and elegant …

Paula: Like a glamorous piece of shit.

Rolando: And, as usual, I hit 'Space' first.

Maria: So I went to this 'Space' club, I had never been before but that's where he wanted us to meet …

Paula: A shitty feeling. Because she went away with this guy for good. So I went straight to the first club I could think of. To 'Space'.

Music. They start to dance. The lighting should suggest a club. Paula is dancing wildly. Maria is feeling shy. Rolando economically keeps time with the beat.

SCENE 2: Inside the club.

The music stops as they start to speak.

Maria: And I just couldn't figure out why the hell he wanted to meet me there. It was full of kids jumping up and down, dancing like zombies … I think he was trying to wind me up. The gynaecologist was playing with me. Or maybe it was a misunderstanding. Was it 'Space' or 'Face'? 'Face' or 'Space'?

Rolando: And it was obvious that this night was going to be just like every other night. Fuck it, I felt like going home the minute I got in the door, but I went to the bar, as usual, and I asked for a Red Bull. I was sitting on a stool, trying to look cool and relaxed and sipping Red Bull with a straw. I felt sick.

Paula: And this shitty feeling turned into an über-shitty feeling the minute I sat at the bar.

Music starts up again and stops after a few seconds.

Rolando: And all those unfamiliar faces who looked so very familiar.

Maria: And all these teenagers milling around having a ball. And me, waiting for my gynaecologist. Sitting at the bar.

Paula: A shitty feeling. I wanted to drown myself in all that shit. Sitting at the bar.

Rolando: Right near these two odd-looking bits … creepy and bored …

Paula: Near two bored losers, dull as dishwater …

Maria: Near two regulars, bored and *very* cool … (*Music starts up again and stops*)

Rolando: And I heroically decide to get the fuck out of that place …

Paula: I've gotta get out of this place right now …

Maria: That's it, I've waited too long … (*Music again as they shout into their mobiles*)

Their mobile phones start ringing.

All three: Yeah! What?

Rolando: Shit.

Paula: Shit.

Maria: Fuckin' shit.

Rolando: I don't care what gigs he's got for me. You can take that Big Dick of yours shove it up your ass.

Paula: Listen, I'm absolutely fine … yeah, I'm fantastic actually … So why are you calling me?

Maria: Well maybe you should have thought of that earlier … I've been here half an hour already …

Rolando: Yeah, I'm in 'Space'. No, not alone, I'm actually with two fuck wagons and I'm gonna fuck their brains out all night long.

Paula: I have to go now … yeah, I'm with someone … Oh, you think it's too soon? Well, I don't give a shit!

Maria: No, I'm not coming, I've just met some friends of mine. So you can take your 'Face' and stick it up your arse!

They all hang up.

Maria: What were you saying about … well, you know …?

Rolando: What?

Paula: Fucking. (*Music stops*)

Rolando: It still stands.

SCENE 3

Torches describe a car. Headlights, indicators etc.

Rolando: Yeah. That's how it all started. Out of this ridiculous situation. Ridiculous. Totally ridiculous. That's how I felt when I walked out of 'Space'. There I was with these two slappers that I'd promised to shag. To be honest, I wasn't really feeling up to it.

Maria: How did I get myself into this? That was my first thought, as I left 'Space'. I suppose just once in my life I wanted to be one of those people, free, dangerous and up for anything. So there I was with two total strangers in my car. Two extremely cool, total strangers.

Paula: All night. I'm gonna go at it all night with a guy and a girl. And neither of them is my type … that's fucked up!

Rolando: So I'm starting to imagine that it's going to be like porn, really cheap, cheesy porn; a threesome in a car.

Maria: Madness. Pure madness. Driving silently up Magheru. And I take a good look at this guy's face in the mirror. Jesus, he might be ten years younger but he's exactly the same type. Just as pushy as my gynaecologist. Or maybe it's just me … I'm gonna fuck someone who looks like the gynaecologist. Great!

Rolando: And I'm staring out the window at nothing in particular. But I can still see that woman checking me out in the mirror.

Paula: And I can't take my eyes off his shoes. UK. Definitely. Same as hers. Unisex or something. Still, I think hers were a bit more expensive. That's what I'm thinking. That her shoes were more expensive than his. This guy who's sitting next to me, in the back seat of this car. I'm gonna have a cynical fuck with this guy, but I keep thinking of her. Well, actually what I'm really thinking of is her shoes, the real thing, straight from the UK, where she eventually ran off with that arsehole. They met in a club and it was instant love … just add water.

Rolando: And your one sitting next to me keeps staring at my shoes, it's like she wants to know what brand they are or something. Exactly the kind of stupid slappers who go clubbing looking to chase 'cool' guys like me. *They catch sight of each other in the mirror and laugh nervously.*

Maria: Thank fuck for the music, at least we don't have to talk.

Paula: I'm glad she switched on some tunes, what's there to talk about. *Paula takes some coke.*

Rolando: Brutal sounds! But better than …

Maria: And we start. They take off their clothes without looking at each other. They even touch without looking. And there's nothing fun about this! (*To the other two*) I thought we're gonna have some fun! What the fuck is this?

Rolando: Put your foot down! Let's get out of Bucharest!

Paula: And put on some decent tunes!

Maria: 100 miles an hour. The smell of my sweat mixed up with the smell of their sweat. A terrible feeling of panic. Full-on excitement, at last!

Sex scene between Rolando and Paula. Paula is feeling a bit sick. For a moment, they both look straight ahead, bewildered. A few gestures in flashlight. It's not obvious as to whether they are hitting each other or having sex.

Rolando: Get in the front!

Paula: Fuck that shit! I don't feel like driving.

Rolando: Ok, I'll drive. And I really put the foot down. I roll down the windows. I've always wanted to see some live girl on girl action. Deadly. Absolutely deadly. DJ Big Dick's bitch should see this. She'd love all this spinning and scratching. In this moment …

Paula: And in this ridiculous moment, when myself and this woman are piggin' into each other and she's not even my type.

Maria: In this moment, kissing a woman, well actually, being kissed by a woman … I feel the panic jamming all my thoughts.

Rolando: And in this moment I start crying like a …

Maria: And the panic turns into crying …

Paula: And, shit, shit, shit, I think I'm gonna burst into tears, fuck it …

The Accident. Choreography. Maria suddenly feels violently ill. Paula tries to get Rolando to stop the car. Rolando turns his head. This series of gestures is repeated three times. Then the actors break up the 'car' and perform movements to suggest a crash. At the end of this sequence they throw the torches on the floor. Music stops.

SCENE 4

Maria: All my savings down the drain. So, goodbye, cute little flat. I had to pay a fortune to fix the car because we crashed outside working hours. We were driving at 100 miles an hour. Luckily none of us had been drinking that night. We just went off the road and rolled two or three, actually four times. No big deal, really.

Paula: I was so happy the next day. I couldn't sit still, that's how happy I was. And suddenly, right there, in the hospital, I realized that those two strangers could be, could actually *mean* something. And I had no idea what.

Maria: And I was really glad that they fired me. In fact, it was me who suggested it. I didn't know why, but I was feeling so good … for the first time in a long time, I had this feeling of … I don't know … joy ... And no, it wasn't the sex … that guy, I don't think I was even into him. And I've certainly never been into women.

Paula: I wasn't really into that girl. And I've never been into men.

Maria: And still, I have never felt so …

Paula: But still, I wanted to meet them again …

Maria: The only bad thing was …

Paula: The only shitty thing was …

Rolando: I can't hear anymore. I can't hear voices, loud noises, but I can hear my own breathing. Continuously. A rhythm. I'll never be a DJ. But no, that's not it, I would have never been a big DJ anyway. I wasn't good at anything. I won't be hearing a lot of bullshit from now on … That's one good thing. I don't know why, but it seemed obvious that we had to meet again. Because something happened. Maybe it was the fear we felt. It probably wasn't the sex. Only that silent panic. And anyway, they were the only ones who weren't asking me stupid questions about that night. So …

Maria: I went to 'Space'. I took my parents' car.

Paula: 'What's wrong with trying to meet them again.' So …

SCENE 5: The club

Paula: I went to 'Space'. And I started to wait. *Music starts and stops before Maria speaks.*

Maria: When I got there, she was already waiting at the bar. We didn't speak. We were waiting for him.

Paula: And all that commotion around us was beginning to get on my nerves.

Maria: I felt like strangling all those plastic kids …

Paula: … their shitty music, their shitty DJ, their shitty Britty clothes …

Maria: … their easy lives, their easy smiles, their bouncing around like cretins … *Music starts and stops for Rolando.*

Rolando: They were already waiting for me. And when I got to the bar everything started to spin. I felt like puking. All those 'super-cool' freaks moving, led by something, connected to a rhythm. A rhythm that wasn't the rhythm of my breathing. It was strange …

Maria: It was strange, the way we just stood there, still. All three of us. And all those 'vacant' …

Paula: With their shitty DJ …

Rolando: All those 'connected' …

Maria: With their special 'scene' …

Paula: With their shitty DJ …

Rolando: All the 'elite' …

Maria: All those 'vacant' …

Paula: With their shitty DJ …

Rolando: All those 'connected' …

Maria: With their special 'scene' …

Paula: And their shitty DJ …

Rolando: All those 'ultra-hip', all those fucking 'Made in Europe', all those still water drinking bastards!!!

Music. Very loud. Then stops suddenly.

Paula: I'm trying to imagine all that shit without the sound. No sounds.

Maria: I'm twenty-seven years old and I have a ridiculous life, my three jobs, my parents who are doing my head in, my gynaecologists and my lawyers and my businessmen.

Paula: I'm twenty-five and I'm trying to have fun but I can't even pretend that there's any fun in this.

Rolando: I am twenty-three years old and my life is already fucked up. Not because of the accident. Because I can't find anything that could possibly give me the tiniest amount of pleasure. I am twenty-three and I haven't done anything. And I don't think I ever will. Something I'd really like doing.

Paula: I've got an idea! I'm telling them to follow me. Down the stairs. I'm looking for something. It has to be here. I see it and I'm going straight for it. The power switch. AND I'M REACHING FOR …

Music and choreography to suggest switching off the power. Music stops.

Maria's scream.

SCENE 6: In the car

Maria is sitting on the front seat.

Maria: Jesus. I can't believe you did that. What the fuck is wrong with you?

Paula: How was I to know those losers in the club were going to start a fucking stampede? How was I know they were going to panic?

Rolando: (*Pushing Paula*) What the hell were you thinking?

Paula: (*To Maria*) What about you? Why the fuck did you start screaming?

Maria: (*To Paula*) Are you crazy?! I was scared!!!

Rolando: (*Very angry, to Paula*) Listen to me, that was so not *cool!* So not fucking cool!

Both girls start laughing. Rolando is laughing too. Hysterically. Rolando kisses Paula violently.

They load their torches with batteries to suggest the loading of guns.

Maria: That's how it all started. We went to at least two clubs a night.

Rolando: At last, I'd found something I enjoyed. Serious job satisfaction. Even if it was unpaid. But money wasn't a problem. My Father was always good for a few quid, enough to keep me going. He didn't want me to bother him and his new bit of gee, two years younger than me she was. And speaking of complete slappers, of course we had to visit the club where DJ Big Dick or DJ Big Fuck or whatever they call him was performing …

Maria: Then I gave up my second job. I had to be fresh for the night shift …

Rolando: We soon sussed out that it was a much better buzz to be there when it all kicked off, so one of us stayed on the dance floor and screamed, for maximum panic, while the other two cut the power. We took turns.

While Maria and Paula are calling out the names of the clubs and the supermarkets that they disconnect, Rolando is keeping the 'rhythm' of their actions – ***Rolando:*** *Stop the tempo! Stop the tempo! Stop the tempo! Stop the tempo! Stop the tempo! Stop the tempo! – building to a crescendo that ends when they all shout 'STOP!'*)

Paula: 'Spell'!

Maria: 'Energy'!

Paula: 'Fever'!

Maria: 'Fire'!

Paula: 'Y Knot'! *Repeat 4 or 5 times each time gathering volume and momentum. They use their torches as guns illuminating each other.*

Maria: We should go outside Bucharest sometimes! All those other cities, think of all those clubs …

Paula: Sure. Let's not be elitist about it.

Maria: We'll dedicate this weekend to the provinces!

Paula: What about this – let's do a tour of the supermarkets. Metro!

Maria: The Mall!

Paula: Prisma!

Maria: Cora!

Paula: Carrefour!

***Maria:** Yeah, yeah. And in McDonald's cute little house. Let's scare the McShit out of them!*

All three: STOP!

SCENE 7

Paula: Sometimes I think that the whole disconnecting idea was already out there. Seriously. Everywhere you go, it's all around you 'get in the loop', 'get plugged in', 'click here', 'send a text', 'join the big fucking party'. All day long, on and on. Until something in you snaps and you say, 'Take your connections and shove them up your hole. I'm too fucking connected. I'm too fucking switched-on. What if I just fucking switched-off?'

Maria: The reason I got three jobs was … well, my parents wouldn't like a loser living in the house. They wanted me to be a big success, you know, like your one … 'Rexona' ultra-dry pits 25 hours a day. The breadwinner. For fuck's sake, the more I brought in, the higher their standards: wide screen TV, flat screen TV, plasma TV and a fridge that shits ice-cubes! Only the latest models. I can't bear to go home in the evening and find out what other shit they've seen in some stupid ad. Shit they don't need but that they'd kill to get. I love them, yeah, I do but … but sometimes … yeah, sometimes I feel like gouging their fucking eyes out.

Rolando: The only thing that stops the rhythm of my breathing is the panic and what happens afterwards … I'm afraid to call it love. Simply because it just might not be that. It could be a kind of madness. And as long as we don't give it a name, we can still hope it'll last. For a while. I don't like using big words … they won't come … but, in the end, I think it's the most real thing that's ever happened to me.

Paula: Three years ago I got a job in an advertising agency, sorry, consultancy. So I've been a creative director, brand manager, executive creative artistic director assistant senior manager group chief executive artistic creative director WHATEVER … In the end I chose copywriting. That's what I really liked doing. It was perfect. The money kept pouring in, the contracts kept coming, and two months ago I quit. One morning, our boss comes in and tells us: 'We're promoting a new product, a wonder laxative, it's going to be an all channel TV ad and the brief goes like this: 'We take a mother … generous, voluptuous, motherly, almost hysterically zealous, but friendly, and she's serving this incredible laxative for breakfast to the entire family cut to them all singing, smiling and jumping around' … I couldn't take it anymore. For three years I had been 'selling': the clean, dry, protection sensation mother, the wrinkle-free mother, the dandruff-free mother, the orgasm shampoo mother, the terrorizing her husband for a piece of chocolate mother, the firm breasted mother, the care-free mother, the nought percent interest mother, the food dancing around the kitchen mother, the doesn't have to do a thing mother, the I'm shagging Mr. Proper mother, la la la la la la la, la la la la la! The mother, the mother sells!

Maria: Wouldn't it be funny to go into work some day and play a little bit with the switchboard? They're such idiots in there they'd never realize it was me.

Paula: If you could get a switchboard and connect it to all the shit in some people's heads, I'd switch the fucker off, to stop the shit from spreading.

Rolando: If all of Romania was connected to one massive switchboard, I'd find it and blow the shit out of it.

We hear the Romanian national anthem. Without words. Rolando and Maria are holding the tune while Paula improvises with the melody switching from jazz to opera etc.

The following poems are recited as a parody of patriotic poems as in a school room.

Rolando: I hang on
To this shining land
With bloody claws
With the spasms of a lunatic.
Like a Siberian tiger
Clinging to the ice.
Like a sad
Whining
Beast.
I'm hanging
onto our shining motherland
With these bloody claws
A convulsing madman
a siberian tiger
who clings to the ice
a sad
Pitiful
Cannibal

Paula: And
Momma's gonna make atomic bombs
For me
Momma's gonna rock me
In a submarine
Momma's gonna restage nine eleven
For me
Remake that B-movie, tape the repeats
For me
Momma's gonna mine the unconscious sea
With my face
Momma's gonna fix it so my poems
replace
All Al-Qaeda's secret tapes.

Mama's gonna hide me in the mountains
And she will put death cars and women
At my disposal
Mama's gonna flow inside my vein
Hallucinogenic fluid killing pain
And she will put death cars and women
At my disposal.

Maria: Fat slaves
Cocooned in silk
Their mistakes hidden
In an SS file
Pig-brained
Living in palaces
Drunk with success
Wallowing in luxury and excess
Nobody can touch them but God.

(They begin to sing the national anthem again until:)

Rolando: ENOUGH! – I scream
And then I stop; abruptly.
I'm no Sandokan
I'm a psychopathic
Child of a beast
Fed on Napalm
Dead from the start –
There was no solution
I'm the bear from the garbage
And the footage of the revolution.

SCENE 8: In the car

Paula is driving, Maria and Rolando are reading the newspapers.

Maria: Listen, there's no way I'm going to 'Spell' for the third time.

Paula: Then you'll have to go to 'Twice' for the fifth time!

Rolando: (*Still reading the paper*) Man, there's nothing going on! What the fuck, have we really gone through every club in Bucharest?

Paula: It would be cool if … but no, I don't know if we're technologically advanced enough …

Maria: For what?

Paula: To disconnect all the TV channels, and we have to do it some time when everyone's glued to the telly!

Maria: (*To Rolando*) Yeah, what about that? We could pull the plug on all those TV stars and their fake tans, all those pompous little bastards …

Rolando: We'd need at least a year to plan a scam like that. So let's start working on it right now. A noble enterprise like this needs to be planned meticulously.

Maria: But, listen when we do this, if we do this, could I do something really special for my parents?

Paula: Feel free …

Maria: Could we cut it off during Andreea Marin's show*?

Paula: Why her?

Maria: Because every time we watch that stupid bitch with her perfect hair interviewing some sad fucker, my Mother tells me to take her as an example …

Rolando: Done! Wait a minute! I think I know a way that we could expand our empire even quicker. Have you ever been to the theatre?

Maria: Once or twice. Last time I went was with the gynaecologist.

Paula: Ages ago, when I was in college. But if I had to choose between a movie and …

Rolando: A girl convinced me to go to the theatre once, she said it was 'reeeally iiinteresting', that's exactly what she said, 'reeeally iiiiinteresting'. We saw the show, I took her home, we kissed goodnight and I never called her again. Jesus, it was brutal, the guys on stage, I couldn't understand a word they said and it sounded like they were about to come half the time … it was unbearable. So I guess they deserve a visit.

Maria: Why? Where's the buzz in that?

Rolando: It's not about our buzz, this way it's about their buzz … Wait, there's something in this paper ... it's mad … there's

* Andreea Marin – flashy and glamorous presenter of a very popular weekly show on TVR 1 (the Romanian National Television).

this guy, wait a second, Theo Herghelegiu*, he's a theatre director. He wrote this letter, here it is, to the Minister of Culture: 'Dear Minister, according to my humble knowledge, the communist regime has fallen (Or maybe not?!) …'

Maria: Yeah, whatever.

Rolando: 'Therefore, I don't see why the Minister of Culture (through his representatives) should make threats such as "if you make this letter public, you can kiss your funding goodbye, forever, and any contracts in any of the companies under our jurisdiction."'

Maria: You can kiss your funding goodbye?!!! Ha ha ha!!! Unbelievable! And what does your man Theo say about that?

Rolando: He says – oh, actually Theo happens to be a woman, she says, what do I have that you could possibly take (something about horses and bicycles).

Maria: Theo rules!

Paula: Well, that's it. She's convinced me, tonight we're going to the theatre.

Maria: (*To Rolando*) Which theatre though?

Rolando: Does it matter? (*He finds an article in the newspaper*) Hey, hold on a second! 'A strange phenomenon has struck at the heart of some of Bucharest's best-known businesses. A group of people, enemies of the law, have been cuttting off the

---

* Theo Herghelegiu: a young Romanian theatre director, notorious for her struggle against the absurdity and arrogance of the authorities who control the theatre system.

power in various clubs, supermarkets etc. creating panic among customers and staff alike.'

Paula: That's us. Hey, we're famous.

Rolando: 'The security services are prepared to take all necessary measures to counteract this … blah, blah, blah.' (*They are all very happy*) Deadly! At last those morons finally got the message.

Maria: I don't see what's so deadly about it. My parents are going to find out now, I could lose the only job I've got left …

Paula: Are you thick?! They're afraid of us!

Maria: You think so?

Paula: Absolutely! They're shitless.

Maria: Okay. Okay. Well if they're afraid of us … Jesus, I feel like I'm in 'Natural Born Killers' or something! That's exactly how I feel!

SCENE 9

From the 'Romanian Nightmares' cycle

The three actors will read all the information on their identification cards. The last words are: ROUMANIE, ROMÂNIA, ROMANIA.

Rolando: (Reading from his ID card) Ministry of Internal Affairs. Identity Card. 1791007440067. SAALLZZNNNNNC. Surname: MATSANGOS. First name: ROLANDO. Parent's name: PROKOPIS, GEORGETA. Serial No: GN807038. Valid Until: 6th of June 2004. ROUMANIE, ROMANIA, ROMÂNIA.

Paula: Carte d'identité. Identity card. Serial No: GL335813. PIN: 2790330170355. Surname: Gherghe. First Name: Paula, dash, Mona, dash, Lisa. Parent's Name: MIHAI, MARIANA. Place of Birth: District of Tulcea. Sex: F Romania.

Maria: Identity Card. Serial No: KL090737. PIN: 2780104510025. Surname: OBRETIN. First Name: MARIA, dash, CRISTINA. Parent's Name: dash, Lidia. Place of Birth: District of Călărași. Romania.

Rolando: I can see your knickers, ROMANIA
'cause you're sitting at the back of the tram
Where it's so easy to see knickers
Only you're not wearing any, ROMANIA
Your specs and your fancy clothes are pointless,
You don't see nothing ROMANIA!

Paula: I pretended I was looking at the blue sky
Through that tram window at Heroes Station
I pretended not to see you, ROMANIA
I pretended not to see the bruise on your ankle.

Rolando: You don't know yet how it's going to be with us, ROMANIA
I'll tell you to gag and you'll gag!

Maria: Will you bet it all on black Romania?
Did you learn how to turn that trick?
Your presidents are cretins, Romania
Your government are a bunch of cretins.

Paula: Romania!
There are people who go crazy for your playmoney
What you did to my Mother,
I know you'll do it to me
I can't even look in your eyes

Rolando: But I shoot my sperm into Coke bottles Romania
Just to remain in your womb
Child of yours eternal and cretin.

Paula: I hope you're happy, Romania

Maria: I hope you're enjoying your nap

Paula: I don't believe you cry, Romania

Rolando: I don't believe I'm your little boy.

SCENE 10: In the car

They are shouting hysterically. Rolando has been hit on the head.

Rolando: Fuck Romanian theatre! Fuck me and my stupid ideas! That's the last time I go to the fucking theatre!

Maria: I didn't see him. Shit! … I didn't see him coming!

Paula: So what the hell were you doing?

Maria: I don't know, I was in the zone … and it was dark for fuck's sake. I don't know, he just came out of nowhere.

Rolando: The fucking bastard hit me on the head!

Paula: Shit. Shit. Shit.

Rolando: I remember falling on the floor and then trying to grab him by the leg.

Maria: Yeah, and there was a hammer, I don't know why there was a hammer there but I took the hammer and I hit him and I hit him and I hit him ...

Paula: You did what? *Looking at Rolando.*

Maria: It was the only thing I could think of! (*Takes the hammer out of her bag*) Here, I took it with me. Now the police won't find the murder weapon. Because, seriously, I hit that guy so hard I might have killed him.

Rolando: He got there just after we pulled the switch. Fuck! … This wasn't supposed to happen.

Maria: What am I gonna do with the hammer?

Paula: Oh stick it up your hole!

Maria: No, no, no, I have to get rid of the hammer. I can't take it home with me!

Paula: Forget about the fucking hammer!

Maria: Maybe he's alive, what do you think? I really didn't hit him that hard! Maybe he just freaked out and fainted!

Rolando: We should have been more careful, that's all.

Maria: If we're caught, I'm out of a job. My boss says yesterday that I look like shit. He wanted to know was I sleeping at night. Because I fucked up a two grand deal, and he's going to take it out of my salary, every month …

Paula: Will you shut the fuck up with your shitty job and your shitty money and your shitty boss!

Maria: I work, you know. Yeah, I have to work for that shitty money. I don't know and I don't give a shit how you earn your money, but I have to work … and … and I'm scared! I'm very fucking scared!

Paula: Well, why didn't you stay at home then? Why didn't you stay at home go to your job, stuff yourself with Xanax and wait for your stupid gynaecologist in some nightclub!

Maria: Get out of my car! Now!

Paula: (*Trying to get out*) Yeah I will. After I've taken a fucking shit in it!

Rolando: What's wrong with you? What the fuck is wrong with you?

Pause.

Paula: I guess we're all freaked out …

Rolando: Ok, here's what we'll do, we'll take a break. Let's meet again in two months.

Paula, Maria: Two months?!?

SCENE 11

Each one of them in a different place.

Maria: That's how it happened, beginning with that night in 'Space' and ending in the theatre. As for that moron, who walked in on us that night, well, he must have had a tough head because we heard he survived. Actually, I think he was more scared than hurt. So, in the end I decided not to destroy the hammer. I kept it as a souvenir. Because I really missed them those two months.

Paula: I wanted to look for them. Not for that … just see them … well, maybe just some shitty pub, in the suburbs … but I realized I never knew what they were doing during the day. Meanwhile, my ex calls me to tell me she's coming back, that she's having some problems adapting to London, blah, blah, blah … The weird thing is even though I was laughing and I was laughing my head off, there was a possibility, just the remotest possibility … that I understood.

Rolando: For two months I listened to the rhythm of my breath. Until I couldn't stand it any more. Then my Father comes and tells me there might be something we could do. Some kind of operation. That they'd put some gizmo in my head and I'd hear like I used to. And all it'd cost was twenty grand. Yeah, he promised he'd get that money for me. Soon. He couldn't understand when I told him I was ok the way I was. He probably thought I was trying to piss him off. I don't give a shit what he thought.

Maria: I couldn't believe they were off it for two months.

Paula: There's no way they did cold turkey for two months.

Rolando: Of course we met. First time was after a week. I was doing my thing. In and out of the clubs ... well, to be honest, I was looking for them.

Maria: Two months … But that didn't mean we couldn't just bump into each other …

Paula: Of course we couldn't talk to each other.

Maria: Well, in those clubs of course … how could you?

Rolando: Of course it was hard to keep myself from going downstairs and pulling … you know …

Maria: At the start of that, I was with some work mates, I wanted to go to the toilet but instead, pure reflex, I went to …

Paula: Of course that's all I was thinking about. I think we all were …

Maria: Actually, we couldn't wait to get it together again …

Paula: All three. Even that dizzy bitch … Shit, I actually missed them.

Rolando: I measured those months by the rhythm of my breath.

SCENE 12: In the car

Maria: I say we take it easy this time. (*Clearly, to Rolando who can't hear*) Easier, easier at the beginning.

Paula: Yeah, okay, maybe we should go and disconnect my grannny so. And don't speak to him like he's thick. He's only deaf.

Rolando: Let's see where we'll start.

Paula: (*Takes out some newspapers, magazines etc*) I don't know what you've been up to for the last few months, but I've been doing my research. And I can now inform you that every week there's some new hot DJ that's the latest thing. BUT, there's this one DJ, and this DJ is it, the bomb, right? All the way from England, coming to the Arena, number three in the world … DJ SASHA! And it's this Saturday. That's three days time.

Maria: Sasha? Who's she?

Paula: She's a he, a guy, a fella, he's number three in the world you thick! And every 'cool motherfucker' in the country is gonna be there. And all the spas from MTV.

Rolando: (*Looking at the paper*) Deadly! DJ Sasha's fucking great.

Paula: Well he deserves a warm welcome then, doesn't he?

Rolando: Listen, I'll buy the tickets, but this time we have to have a serious plan. I'm not joking you, there's going to be the police there and security and stuff.

Maria: Well, it'd be great if we didn't have to kick the shit out of anyone this time.

Rolando: We need to create like a diversion thing … yeah, I know. We call the police and give them a tip-off. But we won't tell them about the Arena. Somewhere else, a club or a shopping centre …

Paula: Sounds good to me. I tell you what, we'll give them the names of four or five clubs.

Rolando: That'll keep them busy so we can do our thing. Who's gonna make the call?

Maria: I am … But only if I get to stay inside with the madness this time.

Paula: Fine. Get out your mobile and call them so.

Maria: Now?

Paula: Yeah!

Maria: (*Into the phone*) Hello! Is this the police? Oh good. Hello. I'm calling to inform about a possible terrorist … I mean, not exactly terrorist, but … wait, wait, there's no need to panic! … Ok, listen this is it – Saturday night, a group of people are planning to cut the power in some of the clubs in Bucharest. You know what I'm talking about? … Four clubs – Onyx, Planters, Spell, Twice … No, they're only going to do them once. The fourth one? Twice. That's the club … twice. No we're only doing it once. Guns? We won't carry any guns, what would they need guns for? … (*Rolando and Paula are making towards her desperate signs to hang up*) What do you mean who am I? I'm a concerned citizen. This is an anonymous phone call so I that's why I'm anonymous. (*Rolando and Paula are getting more and more desperate*) You know what Police, why don't you go fuck yourself ! (*Hangs up. As if she is surprised and delighted that he is a:*) Pervert!

SCENE 13

Paula: At last! Two months of banging our heads off the wall, but we're finally moving again. The funkiest disconnection project we'd ever thought of. Well, that's not counting our TV stations idea, but that'll have to wait a bit.

Rolando: The only thing I've been hearing for two months is the sound of my own breath. Faster and faster. And my brain is about to burst. But I know, the moment I pull that plug, it'll stop. And a fab silence will follow. And all the waiting will be worth it.

Maria: Panic! Panic! And the darkness.

Paula: And panic, panic, panic and silence and silence and silence and darkness and darkness.

They switch their torches. Darkness. Rolando lights a match. During this scene he lights a succession of matches and lets them burn to the end.

Rolando: We're close to ground zero,
To the embryos of icebergs
Floating in space.

Paula: Life has changed
And is coming to an end.

Maria: Each day we're closer
To nobody and no one.
And that's the way it should be.
Nobody's on TV today
Talking about nothing.

Paula: No diploma could guarantee
No one's intelligence.

Nobody's wrapped in diplomas
When talking about nothing.

Rolando: The big cartel presses into every mind
Its filthy fingerprints
And the piano of my heart
beats out this tinny fairground tempo.

Maria: Two billion people blethering every day
Caught in the entrails of the Chat.
They're trying to convince me
That it's all orchestrated by God.

Paula: A billion cars spew
Their poisonous scent in the air.
A couple more zeros
Buys and sells the earth.

Rolando: All of humanity marches forward
Blinder than the blindest mole
To hell, to the witch's brew
TO THE HORRIBLE EXPLOSIVE FINALE.
TO ROMANIA. *Rolando blows out his match.*

SCENE 14: In a club

Music in the background.

Maria: When I got into this thing, I had three jobs and I was hoping to buy a house and a car. Now I don't have a job, I'm living off my parents and I have to take the bus because I can't afford the petrol. No, I wasn't fired. I just gave up working. Because I don't have time anymore. All day and all night I wander through clubs, superstores, cinemas, theatres ... Well, 'wander' isn't the word for it. I'm rushing. Rushing through the clubs. I'm waiting for a sign. (*Beat*) That night, our plan almost worked. They were caught just as they got the switchboard open. At least that's what they said on TV: that they got scared and they electrocuted themselves. Or maybe it was an accident. But, of course, I didn't believe a word of it. I'm sure they managed to find their way out through the darkness. Because they did pull that switch. And that's the only thing that matters, after all isn't it? It was the wickedest panic we'd ever created. So, here I am, in a club, waiting for their signal. They probably decided to lie low for a while and they didn't have time to tell me that. They'll show up eventually. All that I can do is keep on searching through the clubs. Because we still have a lot of projects planned for **ROMANIA** ... *The music stops suddenly. Lights out.*

The End